THE AUTHOR

Kisshōmaru Ueshiba, Aikidō Dōshu, was born in 1921, the third son of Morihei Ueshiba, the Founder of aikidō. He graduated from Waseda University in 1946, became master of the Aikidō Headquarters Dōjō in 1948, and in 1967 was named chairman of the Aikikai Foundation, the principal aikidō organization in Japan and overseas. His formal appointment as successor to his father took place in 1969. He holds several important posts related to the martial arts and is a trustee of the Nippon Budokan, the hall of the martial arts in central Tokyo.

The Spirit of Aikidō

Kisshōmaru Ueshiba

trans. by Taitetsu Unno

KODANSHA INTERNATIONAL
Tokyo • New York • London

Distributed in the United States by Kodansha America, Inc., 575 Lexington Avenue, New York, N.Y. 10022, and in the United Kingdom and continental Europe by Kodansha Europe Ltd., 95 Aldwych, London WC2B 4JF. Published by Kodansha International Ltd., 17-14, Otowa 1-chome, Bunkyo-ku, Tokyo 112-8652, and Kodansha America, Inc. Copyright © 1984 by Kodansha International Ltd. All rights reserved. Printed in Japan.

LCC 83-48881
ISBN 0-87011-850-1
ISBN 4-7700-1350-7 (in Japan)

First edition, 1984
First paperback edition, 1987
00 01 02 15 14 13

CONTENTS

Foreword

Down through the centuries religions have espoused love and compassion and philosophies have taught reverence for life. But we are today faced with an escalating violence which seems to have its own momentum beyond any human control. The world is filled with irreconcilable divisions between friend and foe, good and evil, the oppressor and the oppressed. Violence is used to suppress, break, and eliminate the adversary. When that is accomplished, it searches for another opponent. When will the cycle of violence stop? How can the divisions that separate people be overcome? Where is the power to heal the wounds of pain and suffering?

It is of no small interest that we find in Japanese history a tradition of fighting arts (*bugei*), originally devised to inflict injury and death on the battlefield, transformed into the Way of martial arts (*budō*), dedicated to perfecting the human self by integrating mind, body and spirit. Starting in the early seventeenth century, the Way of the sword transformed the sword that kills into the sword that protects life. This Way of martial arts is consistent with the Way of the tea ceremony, Way of poetry, Way of calligraphy, Way of the Buddha, and innumerable other Ways which in their pure form have provided spiritual sustenance for the Japanese people.

The training and discipline common to all the Ways, martial or cultural, consist of three levels of mastery: physical, psychological and spiritual. On the physical level mastery of form (*kata*) is the crux of training. The teacher provides a model form, the student observes carefully and repeats it countless times until he has completely internalized the form. Words are not spoken and explanations are not given; the burden of learning is on the student. In the ultimate mastery of form the student is released from adherence to form.

This release occurs because of internal psychological changes taking place from the very beginning. The tedious, repetitious and monotonous learning routine tests the student's commitment and will power, but it also reduces stubbornness, curbs wilfulness, and eliminates bad habits of body and mind. In the process, his or her real strength, character and potential begin to emerge. The spiritual mastery is inseparable from the psychological but begins only after an intensive and lengthy period of training.

The heart of spiritual mastery is this: the ego self becoming the egoless self. In every martial and cultural art free expression of self is blocked by one's own ego. In the Way of swordmanship the student's mastery of stance and form must be so total that there is no opening (*suki*) for the opponent to enter. If an opening does occur, it is created by one's ego. One becomes vulnerable when one stops to think about winning, losing, taking advantage, impressing or disregarding the opponent. When the mind stops, even for a single instant, the body freezes, and free, fluid movement is lost.

The Zen monk Takuan (1573–1645), who was a confidant of Yagyū Munenori (1571–1646), master swordsman of the House of Tokugawa, wrote in a short treatise, *The True and Wondrous Sword of Tai-a*:

> The art of the sword consists of never being concerned with victory or defeat, with strength or weakness, of not moving one step forward, nor one step backward, of the enemy not seeing me and my not seeing the enemy. Penetrating to that which is fundamental before the separation of heaven and earth where even yin and yang cannot reach, one instantly attains proficiency in the art.

Tai-a is a mythical sword that gives life to all things, both self and other, protagonist and antagonist, friend and foe.

Yagyū Munenori himself stresses the overcoming of ego through self-discipline in the art of swordsmanship. In a treatise known as *The Household Transmission on the Art of Fighting* he writes that the goal of training in the martial arts is to overcome six kinds of disease: the desire for victory, the desire to rely on technical cunning, the desire to show off, the desire to psychologically overwhelm the opponent, the desire to remain passive in order to wait for an opening and the desire to become free of these diseases.

Ultimately, physical, psychological and spiritual mastery are one and the same. The egoless self is open, flexible, supple, fluid, and dynamic in body, mind and spirit. Being egoless, the self identifies with all things and all people, seeing them not from its self-centered perspective but from their own respective centers. In a circle of limitless circumference every point becomes the center of the universe. The ability to see all existence from a non-self-centered perspective is central to the Shintō identity with nature and also constitutes what Buddhism calls wisdom, which in its highest expression is none other than compassion.

Such a way of thinking is the essence of all the martial and cultural Ways in the Japanese tradition. Aikidō is a modern formulation of this essence, perfected by the genius of Master Ueshiba Morihei (1883–1969). Explaining the intention of his art in a lecture he once gave to a general audience, he stated:

> Budō is not a means of felling the opponent by force or by lethal weapons. Neither is it intended to lead the world to destruction by arms and other illegitimate means. True budō calls for bringing the inner energy of the universe in order, protecting the peace of the world and molding, as well as preserving, everything in nature in its right form. Training in budō is tantamount to strengthening, within my body and soul, the love of *kami*, the deity who begets, preserves and nurtures everything in nature.

Master Ueshiba constantly emphasized that a martial art must be a procreative force, producing love which in turn will lead to a creative, rich life. This was the conclusion to his lifelong quest as a man dedicated to the martial arts. In one of his final talks, he proclaimed: "Aikidō is the true budō, the working of love in the universe. It is the protector of all living things; it is a means by which everything is given life, each in its respective place. It is the creative source of not only the true martial art but of all things, nurturing their growth and development."

Aikidō, being a form of traditional martial art, realizes this universal love through rigorous training of the body. The hard, physical discipline, however, cannot be separated from mental development and real spiritual growth. While many people may fall short of this goal, the crucial element is the process of training, which is beginningless and endless. And while on that path, in a most unexpected moment, the ultimate realization of aikidō as the Way of life—beyond any martial art—may dawn.

It is our good fortune that Master Ueshiba's son and heir, Ueshiba Kisshōmaru, the present head (Dōshu) of aikidō, has consented to this English translation of his original work in Japanese. His concern is that the pure essence of aikidō, unadulterated by competitive egos, either personal or national, be kept firmly at the center of training and practice. After all, *dōjō*, "the place of enlightenment," is a word derived from the Sanskrit *bodhimanda*, the place where the ego self undergoes transformation into the egoless self.

TAITETSU UNNO

Preface

The recent expansion of aikidō on a world-wide scale is nothing less than phenomenal. The total aikidō population today exceeds one million, and the International Aikidō Federation is growing stronger than ever. The reason for this lies in aikidō itself, which, I believe, expresses in both principle and practice the highest form of martial-aesthetic-spiritual art that traditional Japanese culture has produced.

Aikidō manifests the ultimate reality: the flowing spontaneous movements of nature within which is packed the unmatched power of *ki*. Its goal is the formation of the ideal human self unifying body and mind, realized through vigorous mental and physical training, and the attainment of dynamic life in both activity and stillness. The spirituality of its fundamental principle and the rationality of its execution are at the core of aikidō's international renown.

Accompanying the dramatic developments in science, technology and material civilization in modern times is the aggravation of the human spirit, which experiences restlessness, insecurity and loss of direction. This is heightened by the threat of nuclear holocaust; mankind today stands on the brink of global disaster.

In this age of radical dehumanization aikidō has a special attraction. Especially appealing is the fact that each person, regardless of age, sex or athletic ability, can realize through practice the unification of the fundamental creative principle, *ki*, permeating the universe, and the individual *ki*, manifested in breath-power. This unification is the source of life energy, which not only fills the spiritual vacuum but provides daily living with real substance and meaning.

The Japanese martial arts were inspired originally by the goal of victory on the battlefield. But victory is short-lived; it passes quickly and disappears. One may exult in the battle that is won, but this is never the final fulfilling victory. Thus, a contradiction existed: dedicating one's life to training vigorously for a goal that was evanescent.

This contradiction was resolved in the formation of budō (the Way of the martial arts), its foremost modern exponent being aikidō. Aikidō teaches the way to realize absolute victory based on the philosophy of non-contention. Non-contention means to deflate the aggressive, combative, destructive instincts within a person and to channel them into the power of creative love. Such a philosophy carries that much more weight when taught by a martial art, but it is the essence of budō.

Due to the rapid expansion of aikidō throughout the world, we feel that the true meaning of this art has not always been properly conveyed and practiced. Although we welcome the internationalization of aikidō, if it does not preserve the basic philosophy and ideals as formulated by the founder, Master Ueshiba Morihei, it would be indeed regrettable. For this reason we feel a strong sense of responsibility, and we are constantly working to improve the situation.

It is most timely that my work, *Aikidō no kokoro*, has now been translated into English as *The Spirit of Aikidō* by Professor Taitetsu Unno of Smith College, who is a long-time student of aikidō. The original Japanese edition was published in 1981 to commemorate the Fiftieth Anniversary of the Aikidō Headquarters Dōjō. The work contains many traditional Asian views and ideals, some of which may be difficult to grasp. But it is my hope that its central idea, a dynamic life based on the unity of universal and personal *ki*, will be realized through training and practice.

My wish is that this small work may be of benefit especially to students of aikidō, but if the general reader can also gain some understanding of aikidō as a sophisticated art form, contributing not to violence but to harmony in the world, I shall be most grateful.

The Ki of the Universe and Individual Ki

The Uniqueness of Aikidō

Aikidō is essentially a modern manifestation of the Japanese martial arts (*budō*). It is orthodox in that it inherits the spiritual and martial tradition of ancient Japan, first recorded in the eighth-century literary and historical works, *Kojiki* (Record of Ancient Matters) and *Nihongi* (Chronicle of Japan). This does not mean that aikidō blindly carries on the tradition of the ancient fighting arts, merely preserving and maintaining its original form in the modern world.

The ancient fighting arts are a historical and cultural legacy, originating on the battlefield in periods of civil strife and later formalized as budō, the Way of martial arts, in the Tokugawa period (1603–1868). They need to be properly assessed and appreciated. In their original form they are unacceptable to people today and are out of place in the modern world, which in the case of Japan begins with the Meiji Restoration (1868).

The Founder of aikidō, Master Ueshiba Morihei, was born on December 14, 1883. Living in the turbulent time of Japan's modernization, he dedicated himself to establishing a martial art that would meet the needs of contemporary people but would not be an anachronism. The following factors were at the core of Master Ueshiba's primary concerns: an abiding love for traditional martial arts, the care that it not be misunderstood and a deep wish to revive the spiritual quality of budō. He sought to achieve his goal through a relentless quest, given substance by constant training in the martial arts, for the truth of budō throughout the vicissitudes of modern Japanese history.

Ultimately, Master Ueshiba concluded that the true spirit of budō is not to be found in a competitive and combative atmosphere where brute strength dominates and victory at any cost is the paramount objective. He concluded that it is to be realized in the quest for perfection as a human being, both in mind and body, through cumulative training and practice with kindred spirits in the martial arts. For him only such a true manifestation of budō can have a raison d'être in the modern world, and when that quality exists, it lies beyond any particular culture or age. His goal, deeply religious in nature, is summarized in a single statement: the unification of the fundamental creative principle, *ki*, permeating the universe, and the individual *ki*, inseparable from breath-power, of each person. Through constant training of mind and body, the individual ki harmonizes with the universal ki, and this unity appears in the dynamic, flowing movement of ki-power which is free and fluid, indestructible and invincible. This is the essence of Japanese martial arts as embodied in aikidō.

Through the genius of Master Ueshiba the first principle of budō, as formulated by him—the constant training of mind and body as a basic discipline for human beings walking the spiritual path—was transformed into a contemporary martial art, aikidō. Today, it is found in all levels and classes of society and is embraced by countless people all over the world as the martial discipline most suited to our age.

That aikidō is a modern budō does not simply mean that a traditional martial art has taken on contemporary features found in the other "modernized" forms of budō, such as judo, karate and kendo. While inheriting the spiritual aspects of martial arts and emphasizing the training of mind and body, the others have emphasized competition and tournaments, stressing their athletic nature, placing priority on winning, and thus securing a place in the world of sports.

In contrast, aikidō refuses to become a competitive sport and rejects all forms of contests or tournaments, including weight divisions, rankings based on the number of wins and the crowning of champions. Such things are seen as fueling only egotism, self-concern and disregard for others. A great temptation lures people into combative sports—everyone wants to be a winner—but there is nothing more detrimental to budō, whose ultimate aim is to become free of self, attain no-self, and thus realize what is truly human.

This is not intended as a criticism of other martial arts for becoming modern sports. Historically, this direction was inevitable for their survival, especially in Japan immediately after World War II, when all martial arts were banned by the Allied Occupation authorities. Even as sports, they have attracted the interest of many people, whether as participants or spectators. This is positive, for there is no denying that the young, especially, are attracted to martial arts because of the contests and tournaments which decide the best in the field. Despite this trend, aikidō refuses to join their ranks and remains true to the original intention of budō: the training and cultivation of the spirit.

Within the world of aikidō voices calling for tournaments have occasionally been heard, the argument being that it is necessary to gather a wider audience for survival in the present age. In fact, some aikidō practitioners have started independent schools advocating "competitive aikidō." This is a serious matter, since the transformation of aikidō into another form of modern sport could lead to its inclusion in the national sports meets and, in the future, perhaps the Olympic Games.

Aikidō draws a clear and sharp demarcation line from such thinking, and the reason is very clear. Aikidō seeks to maintain the integrity of budō and to transmit the spirit of traditional martial arts, remaining true to the first principle of budō, as enunciated by Master Ueshiba: the constant training of mind and body as the basic discipline for human beings walking the spiritual path.

In the tradition of budō strict adherence to the Founder's ideals and commitment to the Way take precedence over all other considerations. The very reason for aikidō's existence in the present world is because of its identification with the ideals of Master Ueshiba, even though the public may regard it as merely another form of combative martial art.

The unique place claimed by aikidō, clearly differentiating it from both classical budō and its modern counterparts, cannot be truly appreciated by the stereotypes people have of the fighting arts. This fact, together with the principles and movements unique to aikidō, may present some obstacles to the popularization of this art.

At one time or another all practitioners have been asked the question, "What is aikidō?" Even advanced students have difficulty in providing a straightforward answer. Moreover, people who see aikidō movements and techniques for the first time are confounded or skeptical and have many doubts and questions. Such people fall into either one of two groups.

The first group consists of those who watch aikidō with certain assumptions about martial arts, based upon what they have heard or read. On seeing aikidō demonstrations their general reaction is one of disappointment, because they expect to see a display of brute force, combat, violence—and even lethal techniques. At first glance aikidō, with its beautiful flowing movements, appears to be non-violent, even passive. Frequently overheard are such comments as: "Everything seems to be choreographed and planned." "There's no climax, no high point, in the movements." "In a critical situation it would be useless," and so on. These criticisms are understandable and come especially from the young who seek thrills in victory and conquest or from those who have stereotypes of martial arts as consisting of shouting, hissing, kicking, hitting and destroying people.

In the second group are those who have become acquainted with modernized martial arts, especially their competitive forms, and view aikidō from that vantage point. Their criticisms are various: "Why doesn't aikidō hold championship tournaments, like judo, karate and kendo?" "Why is it limited to public demonstrations which become boring once you've seen one?" "Since there are no tournaments, it's impossible to tell who is strong and who is weak, who are beginners and who are advanced students." "Without tournaments no one practices and trains seriously." Again, the criticism is understandable, since people generally want to see who has the best technique and who is the strongest.

Another naive but commonly asked question is, "Can one win a fight if he knows aikidō?"

All of these questions and criticisms are simplistic and superficial, revealing ignorance of the basic principle of aikidō and misunderstanding of the chief characteristic of martial arts: the training of the spirit. If a person who has no self-discipline wants to show off his physical prowess and seeks to learn aikidō simply for its fighting technique, he will be asked to leave. Without actually practicing aikidō with some patience and experiencing this art firsthand, the questions will never be answered to full satisfaction.

Actual training in aikidō is the only way to grasp its significance and to gain some benefit, tangible or intangible. Most aikidō practitioners have gone through such a process—beginning with doubts and questions, being initiated into practice, then gradually becoming acquainted with the method and form of aikidō. Later, they experience its irresistible attraction and finally some measure of realization of its bottomless depth. A person who has gone through this cycle will have learned several things about aikidō that make it a unique martial art.

First, he will be surprised. Unlikc thc "soft" appearance seen in public demonstrations, it can actually be "hard," vigorous and dynamic, with powerful wrist locks and direct strikes (*atemi*). Contrary to what one might assume, aikidō contains several devastating techniques, especially those meant to disarm and subdue the enemy.

Next, he will be shocked to discover, even at the beginner's level, how complicated and difficult it is to execute the basic techniques and movements, such as taking a fall (*ukemi*), proper distancing (*ma-ai*), entering (*irimi*) and other body movements (*tai-sabaki*). The fact is that the whole body, not just the arms or legs, must move continuously in a coordinated manner, and this must be done with speed, vigor and power. In order to perform smoothly and swiftly, an extraordinary degree of mental concentration and agility, balance and reflex action are necessary.

He will also realize the importance of breath control, which includes normal breathing but something much more that connects with ki-energy. This mastery of breath-power is basic to every move and execution and insures the continuity of flow in the movements. Furthermore, it is intimately connected with the philosophy of budō developed by Master Ueshiba, as we shall see later.

Finally, as the student advances he will be amazed at the endless number of techniques with their variations and applications, all characterized by rationality and economy. It is only after experiencing the complexity of aikidō movements that he will appreciate the centrality of ki, both personal and universal. And then he will begin to sense the depth and sophistication of aikidō as a martial art.

In brief, only through actual training in aikidō does one become fully aware of the crucial dimension of budō—constant training of mind and body as the basic discipline for human beings walking the spiritual path. Only then can one fully appreciate the rejection of contests and tournaments in aikidō and the reason for public demonstrations being a display of constant training, not of ego accomplishment.

Harmonizing Ki

In recent years interest in the ancient principle of ki has increased enormously, but most accounts neglect its philosophical roots. Briefly, the essence of ki is both personal and impersonal, concrete and universal; it is the basic, creative energy or force in life, transcending time and space. We will explore the meaning of ki more fully later. For now we will ask what is the significance of this great surge of interest. I believe that it reflects the deep yearning in contemporary life for some vital principle, some energizing force, that can fulfill and give meaning to existence.

Behind the advances in scientific knowledge and technology, as well as the attendant economic prosperity, exists the hollowness of the human spirit. This seems to be the fate of modern man. We see in the midst of material abundance, artificial comforts and the massive bureaucratization of life, a growing dissatisfaction and frustration underscoring the malaise that is spreading throughout the world. More than ever before in history we need to recover what it means to be truly human and to be truly caring. One of the consequences of this quest is the Western encounter with Asian philosophies and cultures, one aspect of which is the discovery of ki as an integral part of East Asian spirituality. This phenomenon is part of the reason for the Western interest in aikidō, which literally means the Way (*dō*) of harmony (*ai*) with *ki*.

The demand for more knowledge about ki is clearly evident whenever I visit aikidō centers throughout the world. In September, 1978, for example, I travelled to Brazil, Argentina and Uruguay. I recall very clearly the words of the Honorable Luis Panteleon, professor of law and judge of the Sao Paulo district court, who said at that time:

> As a person who sits on the bench and judges people, I was disturbed with the self-concern and materialistic tendencies I found within myself. I joined the Brazil Aikikai when I learned that aikidō was a martial art that represented the essence of Japanese culture. By practicing aikidō I not only dissolved my frustration but also discovered ki, the heart of the human spirit, hidden beneath my superficial self. I felt true joy and gratitude, and I believe I have grown as a human being.

During the welcome reception at the Third Congress of the International Aikidō Federation held in Paris in late September and early October, 1980, President Guy Bonnefond similarly made a significant point. He said, in effect:

> We believe it is only natural that aikidō, representing a highly developed form of martial art and containing the noblest legacy of Japanese culture and spirituality, should be well received in Europe with its high civilization and tradition of knighthood. As a path to unify mind and body, aikidō is a timely gift to our youth, who are slowly losing the spirit of what it means to be human. I wholeheartedly applaud this rare meeting of aikidō and the modern West.

For those of us who have dedicated ourselves to the cultivation of aikidō, quietly, without fanfare or publicity, it brings great joy to hear of its acceptance on an international scale. But we cannot be content with simply rejoicing when we realize the heavy responsibility that lies on our shoulders in trying to meet the expectations of people all over the world. It is a responsibility not to be taken lightly.

One of our major concerns is that aikidō, because of its unique qualities rooted in Japanese spirituality, tends to invite misunderstanding. This tendency increases as aikidō is introduced to peoples of different cultures and lifestyles, not only among beginners who have unrealistic expectations but also among advanced students who may miss its subtle principles and misrepresent them. Both aikidō instructors and students must dedicate themselves to truly mastering the art, plumb its depths, dispel distortions, and present its authentic form. Otherwise, the disappointment of interested people will be great and irreversible. This possibility holds true in Japan as well as in the foreign countries where aikidō is rapidly growing. As far as aikidō techniques are concerned, there may be only minor problems, but the philosophical and spiritual basis of aikidō poses an entirely different challenge. Real problems may arise unless we return to the original teaching of the Founder and clarify the essential meaning of aikidō as fundamentally a matter of the spirit.

At the heart of aikidō as a spiritual way is ki, the world-forming energy which also lies at the core of each human being, waiting to be realized and actualized. While the concept of ki originates with the seminal thinkers of ancient China—Lao-tzu, Chuang-tzu, Huai-nan-tzu, as well as Kuan-tzu, Ch'eng-tzu, Confucius and Mencius—it is not limited to them, for it underwent changes in the evolution of history. The connotation of ki takes on variegated colorings and nuances in the different cultural spheres and time periods of East Asian civilizations. In Japan after this concept was introduced it interacted with the native ethos to form a distinctive world-view, encompassing attitudes to nature, life, death and so on.

The original idea of ki developed as a metaphysical principle in a number of Chinese schools of thought. Ki was, for example, the essential principle of harmony, and it was the source of creativity expressed in the form of yin and yang (Lao-tzu), the vital fullness of life (Huai-nan-tzu), the courage arising from moral rectitude (Mencius), the divine force that penetrates all things (Kuan-tzu).

As a term, it was never clearly defined. Sometimes it was equated to empty space (the void) or nothingness (Lao-tzu), at other times to the formative energy emerging out of chaos (Chuang-tzu). It was regarded by some philosophers as a dualistic principle that structures the universe. That is, the light aspect of ki became Heaven, and the heavenly ki became the sun. Its heavy aspect coagulated to become Earth, and from the earthly ki was born Water. This dualism evolved into the ki operating as yin and yang, darkness and lightness, from which arose the Five Elements Theory and the divinations of the *Book of Changes*.

In the Five Elements Theory, Wood and Fire belong to ki as the light principle, Metal and Water to ki as the dark principle, and Earth is said to be found between the two. Climatic changes and human fortunes could be predicted by the ebb and flow, the harmonious and antagonistic workings of the Five Elements. In the *Book of Changes* the unbroken line (–) symbolized yang and the broken line (– –) yin, and their various combinations produced the eight trigrams—creative, receptive, arousing, gentle, abysmal, clinging, keeping still and joyous. They could be read for divination purposes and various events predicted. Broadly speaking, the principle of ki was associated with the working of yin-yang dualism.

This primarily metaphysical principle of ki was introduced into Japan in the Nara (710–94) and Heian (794–1185) periods and generally upheld, but the introduction of Buddhist thought from India via China affected its meaning, due particularly to the idea of karmic retribution.

More significantly, the idea of ki combined with indigenous views of nature, and it was taken to be the force responsible for the cyclical process of growth, budding, flowering and the withering of plants and trees. Many compound words were formed that are intimately connected with nature's ways: cultivating energy, *yō-ki*; recovering life, *kai-ki*; spirit-energy, *sei-ki* and so on. It was also identified with a powerful, demonic agent that controlled love and hate in interpersonal relationships, and it was incorporated into the magico-religious use of yin-yang, the Five Elements Theory and divination, which are frequently mentioned in Heian literature, such as the *Tale of Genji*.

The most dramatic changes in the interpretation and application of ki began to take place with the rise of the samurai class from the late Heian period. The process continued throughout the Kamakura (1185–1336) and Muromachi (1336–1573) periods, the ensuing century of civil wars, and into the Azuchi-Momoyama period (1568–1603), reaching its apex in the early Tokugawa (1603–1868). The samurai who faced constant threats of death in an age of warfare understood ki in terms of courage, *shi-ki*; will power, *i-ki*; vigor, *gen-ki*; and bravery, *yū-ki*. They were also concerned with equanimity, *hei-ki*, and conserving energy, *shū-ki*, which attempt to prolong breathing, *ki-soku*, as a matter of life and death.

It was during the Tokugawa shogunate, when Japan experienced almost 300 years of relative peace, that great debates on bujutsu were held to provide a theoretical basis for the art of swordsmanship and to prevent its becoming degenerate and lifeless. Those discussions yielded a logical, theoretical treatment of ki, as well as an appeal to its philosophical and spiritual possibilities. In pursuing the latter point a return to the ideas of yin and yang occurred.

For example, in an important text on classical jūjutsu, which is closely connected to modern judo and has affinities with aikidō, we find the following statement taken from *Densho chūshaku*, a work of the Kitō School.

> *Kitō* means rising and falling. Rising is the form of yang, and falling is the form of yin. One wins by recourse to yang and wins

> by recourse to yin. . . . When the enemy shows yin, win by yang. When the enemy is yang, win by yin. . . . To make the mind powerful, utilizing the rhythm between strength and suppleness in technique shows mastery. To discard one's strength and win by using the enemy's strength works because of ki as taught in our school. When one discards strength, one returns to the fundamental principle. If one does not rely on strength but uses ki, the enemy's strength will rebound and he will fall by himself. This is the meaning of winning by using the enemy's strength. You should carefully consider this matter. In brief, the weak overcomes the strong.

To illustrate the importance of ki in the art of swordsmanship we cite the following quotations as being representative views.

> Opportunity for victory is dependent on ki. Carefully observing the enemy's ki and moving in accord with it is called keeping the opportunity for victory before you. In Zen they speak of the "opportunity for manifesting Zen," referring to the same thing. The ki that is hidden and not revealed presents the opportunity for victory. (*Heihō kaden sho*)

> In all matters related to the arts, including martial arts, superiority is determined through training and practice, but true excellence is dependent on ki. The grandeur of heaven and earth, the brilliance of sun and moon, the changing of the seasons, heat and cold, birth and death, are all due to the alternation of yin and yang. Their subtle working cannot be described by words, but within it all things fulfill life by means of ki. Ki is the origin of life, and when ki takes leave of form, death ensues. (*Tengu geijutsu ron*)

Let us now turn to the understanding of ki as conceived by Master Ueshiba. His view of ki, born out of an intuitive insight into the working of the universe, was expressed in pithy, concise language. It is sometimes difficult to grasp his main points, but a meditative reading of what he has to say may give us some clue to his understanding of ki. Two of his statements on ki are:

> Through budō I trained my body thoroughly and mastered its ultimate secrets, but I also realized an even greater truth. That is, when I grasped the real nature of the universe through budō, I saw clearly that human beings must unite mind and body and the ki that connects the two and then achieve harmony with the activity of all things in the universe.
>
> By virtue of the subtle working of ki we harmonize mind and body and the relationship between the individual and the universe. When the subtle working of ki is unhealthy, the world falls into confusion and the universe into chaos. The harmonizing of a united ki-mind-body with the activity of the universe is critical for order and peace in the world.

Master Ueshiba further elaborates on the operation of ki and its necessity for a well-balanced life.

> The subtle working of ki is the maternal source that affects delicate changes in breath. It is also the source of martial art as love. When one unifies mind and body by virtue of ki and manifests ai-ki [harmony of ki], delicate changes in breath-power occur spontaneously and *waza* [proper technique] flows freely.
>
> The change in breath, connected with the ki of the universe, interacts and interpenetrates with all of life. At the same time the delicate breath-power enters into all corners of one's body. Entering deeply, it fills one with vitality, resulting naturally in variegated, dynamic, spontaneous movements. In this way the whole body, including the internal organs, becomes united in heat, light and power. Having accomplished unification of mind and body and being in oneness with the universe, the body moves at will offering no resistance to one's intentions.

Master Ueshiba's conclusion about ki, reached after a lifelong quest for the truth of budō through years of martial discipline and training, becomes increasingly subtle and spiritual as he continues:

> The delicate changes in breath cause subtle movements of ki in the void. Sometimes movements are fierce and potent, at other times slow and stolid. By such changes one can discern the degree

> of concentration or unification of mind and body. When concentration permeates mind and body, breath-power becomes one with the universe, gently and naturally expanding to the utter limit, but at the same time the person becomes increasingly self-contained and autonomous. In this way when breath works together with the universe, the unseen spiritual essence becomes a reality within oneself, enfolding and protecting and defending the self. This is an introduction to the profound essence of ai-ki.

Ki, then, is twofold: the unity of individual-universe and the free, spontaneous expression of breath-power. The former inherits the idea of ki held by the ancient Chinese thinkers, but it is to be realized through unifying ki-mind-body in aikidō training. In the process of training oneness with the ki of the universe is achieved spontaneously without effort. The latter part of the statement teaches that a person's breath controls his thoughts and his bodily movements. When the rhythms of breath and aikidō movements become harmonized with the rhythm of the universe, one's mind and body become centered and every movement becomes a spherical rotation.

The reason for Master Ueshiba's emphasis on the dual functioning of unity and spontaneous expression is that he saw the essence of ki as being the essence of his budō. With this as the starting point, our responsibility is to continue clarifying the ki that is central to aikidō and further develop its significant implications for contemporary life.

The Power of Ki

An aikidō student who has trained regularly should have some personal insights into ki, even if he may not know its historical and theoretical derivation. As outlined in the previous section, ki is an ancient principle which forms the crux of East Asian philosophies and religions. But variations exist in its concrete manifestation in a person, depending on individual temperament, aspiration, physical attributes, experience and background. Thus, differences in the way students feel and think about ki are inevitable.

We may hear students say that "It is a feeling of some kind of energy coming forth from mind and body in harmony." Or "It is a strange, vital power which appears unexpectedly at times from an unknown source." Or "It is the sense of perfect timing and matched breathing experienced in practicing aikidō." Or "It is a spontaneous, unconscious movement which refreshes mind and body after a good workout," and so forth.

Each answer is valid in the sense that it is a true reaction gained through actual personal experience. And being a dircct expression of a felt condition, it contains a certitude that cannot be denied. If this is so, the differences in response are negligible, and the great variety attests to not only the difficulty in precisely defining ki but shows that the depth and breadth of ki defy coverage by a single definition.

While the subject of ki may be treated historically and philosophically, our interest is to approach it through personal experience, training and realization in a martial art. When ki is actualized and confirmed through personal involvement, it leads to the development of character and the wholeness of a person. At the same time, this pursuit of ki leads inevitably to an appreciation of its philosophical and spiritual basis. Ultimately, the proper understanding of ki must be experiential as well as intellectual, and intellectual as well as experiential. This fact is taken into serious consideration when we develop the training curriculum: its method, content and order.

In aikidō training the ultimate goal is the unity of ki-mind-body, but its uniqueness is that movements with the flow of ki are stressed from the very beginning. Special attention is paid to experiencing and mastering ki, so that all movements will be characterized by spherical rotation. Students are taught the unity of ki-mind-body not only through movement, but even prior to any practice of *waza*. They are taught, for example, that ki is concentrated in a stable and strong centrum, the point that is the natural center of gravity (two inches below the navel) when a person stands in a relaxed posture. When ki flows through arms, hands and fingertips, the hands become a weaponless weapon called *te-gatana*, which means literally "sword-hand." Before the practice of any movement, it is customary to cultivate breath-power by an exercise known as *kokyū-hō* (literally, breathing-method), both sitting and standing, and to learn to establish the proper distance (*ma-ai*) between oneself and one's partner.

The main point is that unlike other forms of martial arts, including all classical and modern budō which teach the oneness of mind-technique-body, aikidō stresses ki rather than technique and trains ki-mind-body. Of course, *waza* is consistently practiced but the degree of mastery is dependent upon the degree of unifying ki-mind-body, and this is the sole basis of evaluating proficiency in aikidō.

As we have tried to show, ki is to be understood both experientially and intellectually, but there is another aspect that cannot be neglected by people living in an age of science. The original source of ki is to be found in the world view of ancient China, intimately interwoven with the myth of world formation, and our question is, how does this notion of ki fit into a scientific world view?

When ancient people used their intellectual and imaginative powers to discern the workings of the universe, the source of all life, they came up with the concept of ki. They also tried to explain the order in nature and the cosmos by this principle. The validity of ki as the generative source of life still remains, I believe, but it was deduced from observation of the knowable world and did not involve the unknowable universe.

In our age of science the unknowable universe has become much closer to us, and in fact through scientific means we can actually see and touch what was once far beyond our grasp, even though it may still be but a small portion of the vastness of space. It may be important for us to seek the relationship between ki and the modern scientific view of the universe, because a scientific explanation may be necessary for the acceptance of ki by contemporary people.

Scientific knowledge of the universe began in the late 17th century with Isaac Newton and his theory of universal gravitation as a fundamental law of nature. Since then immense changes and rapid developments have taken place, bringing us to the point where the exploration of the universe has become a routine matter. The modern space era began with Yuri Gagarin, the Russian cosmonaut, who circled the earth on April 12, 1961, in his spaceship, Vostok I. An intense rivalry grew up between Russian and American scientists in space exploration, and on July 20, 1969, American astronauts succeeded in landing on the moon in their Apollo 11 spacecraft, with Neil Armstrong becoming the first human being to set foot on the moon. (The third U.S. astronaut and now U.S. Senator, John Glenn, had a strong interest in aikidō, visited the Hombu Dōjō, and heard Master Ueshiba lecture.) The exploration of the universe continues with space shuttles and satellites, and it may be interesting to see how this will relate to our understanding of ki, but that is a task for the future. For our purposes, however, some preliminary remarks may be in order.

Recently I read the book *Cosmos* by Carl Sagan, the distinguished Cornell astronomer and Pulitzer Prize-winning author. In a special preface for the Japanese edition, Dr. Sagan wrote:

> It was Pythagoras of ancient Greece who first used the word *cosmos* to describe an orderly universe that human beings could understand. There is definitely an order that reigns in the universe. This does not mean that everything is in perfect order, because in the light of scientific research we know the universe is constantly changing and much chaos exists. Nevertheless, the cosmos in which order and confusion coexist has infinite beauty.
>
> Our bodies are made up of the dust from the stars. The same atoms that constitute the stars make up our bodies. We are children of the stars, and the stars are our home. Maybe this is the reason we are entranced with the stars and the Milky Way.

He continues,

> The nitrogen contained in our genes, the calcium in our teeth, the iron in our blood and the carbon in our apple pie were made in the cosmic kitchen that is the star. Our bodies are made up of the particles that constitute the stars. Indeed, in a very profound sense we are children of the stars.

Dr. Sagan concludes that humankind, as the most advanced species on earth, must take great care in engaging in advanced technological experimentations and, as children of the stars, work in harmony with the order that reigns in the cosmos. Also, to be fully cognizant of and act in accordance with the changes and confusions found in the universe is absolutely essential for the survival of our civilization.

Cosmos is not a philosophical treatise, but it contains a wealth of information on the most recent data in space science. And it does remind us once again that the universe is the source of our life and that our lives are intimately connected with its order and change. On this very point, although from entirely different perspectives, there is agreement with the intuitive understanding of life in East Asian thought. The nature of the universe being disclosed by recent scientific discoveries is of a different order—much more complex than the world-view with ki at the center—and it can be understood in totally material terms. But from the standpoint of human beings, our existence and well-being, its ultimate goal can be said to be identical with that of Asian philosophies. With regard to concern for well being, the latter are very clear about the relationship between the individual and the universe. In the words of Master Ueshiba it is to "harmonize the ki of the universe and the ki of the individual, responding to all things from ki, and becoming one with ki."

A difficult question is whether ki can be scientifically established. On this point the concept of biological rhythm advocated by the Nobel Prize winning biologist, Dr. Karl von Frisch, may be suggestive. It does not pertain to ki directly but offers some ideas to consider. According to this theory, in the process of evolution living organisms were influenced by various cyclic changes, and as they synchronized their life to these changes, biological rhythms became implanted or stored as information in the genes. The activities of many organisms, therefore, are expressions of their particular biological rhythm.

Scientists say that biological rhythms extend back to the remote origins of our universe 4.6 billion years ago, when our solar system was first born. The beginnings are found in the rhythm of night and day, resulting from the earth's rotation, and 3 billion years ago this cycle of night and day gave rise to the growth of amoebas. When the separation of land and sea occurred, a great variety of living organisms appeared on earth, and a complex of biological rhythms developed. When our human ancestors began to walk on the face of the earth approximately 2 million years ago, the biological rhythms became very subtle and complicated.

At present it is presumed that the human brain contains 5 billion strands of DNA, demonstrating the complexity of biological rhythms, but we are also told that basic rhythms of nature—night and day, the ebb and flow of tides, meteorological and astronomical happenings—still have the greatest impact upon us.

Although the details of these theories and their validity cannot be easily ascertained, from a intuitive viewpoint we can say that the way we feel and the condition of our minds and bodies is without doubt related to biological rhythms. I also strongly feel that the idea of ki, however naive it may be scientifically, is also connected somehow to biological rhythms.

As a bold hypothesis, I would venture to say that what Master Ueshiba described as the unity of universal ki and individual ki parallels the idea of cosmological rhythm being one with biological rhythm. It may be difficult, or even impossible, to scientifically analyze and measure the achievements of the human spirit, especially if they are realized through insight, intuition or revelation, but it would be foolish not to make the attempt. Otherwise, we may be speaking only esoteric jargon and fall into subjectivism and dogmatism.

Finally, another area of consideration for the future development of the concept of ki is to listen to what foreign students of aikidō have to say on this topic. With the rapid growth of aikidō internationally, the problem of translating key terms into foreign languages appears, but it seems that *ki* is universally accepted as it is in Japanese, whether in Europe, America or Southeast Asia. The perplexing problem is to give even a tentative translation for ki. It may be relatively easy to give a linguistic or analogical explanation. To render ki into a single foreign word is almost impossible.

If a person knows the Japanese language, we can begin to explain ki by referring to its many compounds and convey a general sense of the term. If not, we are forced to come up with a foreign equivalent. Since we lack a precise equivalent, the translation will depend on the emphasis we place on the diverse dimensions of ki. That is, we can stress the spiritual aspect (spirit, soul, ethos), the affective aspect (sense, intuition, feeling), or the psycho-physiological aspect (breathing, breath). If we understand ki as primarily spiritual, we can speak of *spirit* in English, *esprit* in French and *Geist* in German. If we approach it from the affective side, it would be something like *feeling* or *intention* in English and *Stimming* in German. If the psycho-physiological aspect is emphasized it would be close to the Greek *psyche* or English *ether*.

All of these equivalents, while touching upon aspects of ki, still fail to convey its rich and pregnant meaning. This shows that a proper appreciation of ki is impossible without some knowledge of East Asian thought. For this reason we continue to use ki in the original Japanese, regardless of the language of communication, and aikidō students seem to prefer this. Perhaps this is because foreigners are attracted to this unique expression of Japanese cultural and spiritual legacy and seek to grasp its essence through both experiential and intellectual means.

Aikidō knows no boundaries, national, racial or religious. It is open to the world, and it is gratifying to see peoples of different countries all over the world pursuing the path of aikidō together, mutually supporting and stimulating each other. In fact, I often see foreign students whom I respect highly for being more dedicated to aikidō training than their sometimes complacent Japanese counterparts. Although this is a welcome situation, my deep wish is that everyone, Japanese and non-Japanese alike, will seek the heart of aikidō, so that they can manifest not only the *waza* but also the basic philosophy taught by Master Ueshiba. This was his abiding wish for all students:

Aiki is the power of harmony,
Of all beings, all things working together.
Relentlessly train yourself—
Followers of the Way.

Entering and Spherical Rotation

Nen and Mind-body Clarity

As a child, when I learned that the earth was spherical, I imagined undertaking great adventures. I wanted to see whether I would return to the same spot if I moved directly forward and circled the earth, and I thought of tunneling straight through the earth and coming out on the opposite side. I suppose children everywhere have such dreams. Nowadays, with passenger jets circling the globe constantly, we can easily appear on the other side of the earth.

So it was that my childhood dream became a reality when a group of us from the Aikidō Headquarters Dōjō were invited to South America in September, 1978. The occasion was the Seventieth Anniversary Celebration of Japanese Immigration to Brazil. The invitation was extended to us by the Aikidō Federation (R. Kawaii, President), and we received a lively reception in Sao Paulo, Rio de Janeiro and Mogi das Cruzes, where many Japanese live and are influential in the community. The city council of Sao Paulo unanimously voted to confer upon me the distinction of honorary citizenship. This was gratifying, of course, but I was also deeply impressed by the serious and earnest attitude shown by both aikidō practitioners and potential students as they watched the public demonstrations and received instruction during practice sessions.

After our visit to Brazil, we went to Argentina for four days and to Uruguay for two days. Again we held public demonstrations and gave special instruction in aikidō in Buenos Aires and in Montevideo, and, again, in both cities we were overwhelmed by the warm reception we received and the sincere attitude of the aikidō practitioners.

The enthusiasm for aikidō wherever we went was far beyond our expectations, but one of the unforgettable moments was realizing my childhood dream of standing on the other side of the earth, for South America is on the other side of the earth from Japan, and Uruguay is directly opposite Japan.

Our visit to Montevideo on September 24 and 25 was one to be truly cherished, but another equally moving event awaited us. On the day following an aikidō demonstration held in the largest auditorium in Montevideo, built to commemorate independence from Spain, we were invited to the Uruguay Military Academy. This is an elite school with only 300 students, selected from among the brightest young men in the country, and in a curriculum heavily filled with courses in military science aikidō is a regular course. Why was only aikidō included in the curriculum when both judo and karate are also very popular in the country?

At the conclusion of the public demonstration and my lecture on aikidō, the president of the military academy stood up and gave an inspiring speech. He said:

> In the fluid movements of aikidō there is always a firm center. A sense of balance pervades every motion of the hand and foot and they glide smoothly, as if in a dance, because the movement of the whole body is nothing but the smooth movement of the center. I believe the main point in aikidō is the realization of a strong, firm center. What is essential for our country as it faces a turbulent world is to cultivate a spirit having a strong center within and a benevolent form without. I want the students of this academy, who are destined to become leaders of our country, to train hard in aikidō and realize this strong center both spiritually and physically. This is the reason why aikidō is included in our regular curriculum.

The president expressed everything I had been thinking. A strong, firm center is what Master Ueshiba constantly called the unity of ki-mind-body. This is the critical essence of aikidō both in principle and in actual movement. While I was deeply impressed with his address, I was even more determined to fulfill our responsibility as students of aikidō to make sure that this legacy would be made more easily available to everyone, regardless of race or nationality. Aikidō's unique teaching and techniques must always be in accord with the basic essence of aikidō. If we take pride only in its uniqueness and become attached to it, we may fall victim to myopic vision, dogmatism, self-conceit and provincialism. Having come to the opposite side of the earth, unexpectedly I was given the opportunity to reflect on the future of aikidō.

The essence of aikidō, the unity of ki-mind-body, is to be realized by the whole person. If we grasp it merely as a spiritual reality, we may become doctrinaire and fall into abstraction. If we see it only as a matter of technique and physical prowess, then we become satisfied with a simplistic explanation of motor movements. The essence encompasses both the spiritual and physical, and ultimately we must realize it as the budō unifying ki-mind-body from a philosophical and religious point of view.

The best way to properly master this essence is to carefully consider the words of the Founder. His sayings may be somewhat difficult at first reading, but repeated reading and reflection will help to reveal the various levels of meaning contained within them. The frequent reference to the Japanese word *nen* may be bothersome, but we will retain the original term because of the lack of an exact English equivalent. (*Nen* connotes concentration, one-pointedness, thought-moment.) The realization of nen is the key to opening the essence of aikidō; in fact, it constitutes the very heart of aikidō. The following statement by Master Ueshiba clarifies what is meant by this:

> This body is the concrete unification of the physical and spiritual created by the universe. It breathes the subtle essence of the universe and becomes one body with it, so training is training in the path of human life. In training the first task is to continually discipline the spirit, sharpen the power of nen, and unify body and mind. This is the foundation for the development of waza, which in turn unfolds endlessly through nen.
>
> It is essential that waza always be in accord with the truth of the universe. For that to take place proper nen is necessary. If one's nen is connected to the desires of the small self, it is erroneous. Since training based upon erroneous ideas goes against the truth of the universe, it invites its own tragic consequences and eventual destruction.
>
> Nen is never concerned with winning or losing, and it grows

> by becoming properly connected to the ki of the universe. When that happens, nen becomes a supernatural power that sees clearly all things in the world, even the smallest movement of hand or foot. One becomes like the clear mirror reflecting all things, and since one stands in the center of the universe, one can see with clarity that which is off-center. This is the truth of winning without fighting.
>
> To develop the subtle movements of ki based on nen, you must understand that the left side of the body is the basis of martial art and the right side is where the ki of the universe appears. When one reaches the realm of absolute freedom, the body becomes light and manifests divine transformations. The right side brings forth power through the left. The left becomes a shield and the right the foundation of technique. This natural, spontaneous law of nature must be based in the centrum, and one must manifest the self freely as dynamic, spherical rotation.

Master Ueshiba taught that the cultivation of nen was the one-pointed concentration of the spirit as it seeks union with the universal reality that brought us into this life on earth. When the mind-body unified by nen harmonizes with the principle of an ordered universe, a person becomes free of self-centeredness and self-consciousness, giving birth to a supernatural all-seeing power. The person in accord with the principle of universal change moves deftly with lightness and agility, able to freely manifest himself in spherical movements.

Nen, the single-hearted concentration seeking the unity of the order in the universe and the principle of change, becomes the wellspring of the subtle working of ki. When this subtle working, rooted in nen, is manifested in the heart and mind of a practitioner, he becomes free and open, and his insight becomes penetrating. When it works through the body, the result is spirited, dynamic movement in circular and spherical rotation. In short, nen is the line that connects ki-mind-body and the universal ki.

Master Ueshiba's discovery of nen can be ascribed to his relentless training over a period of many years, but it was his experience in critical life-or-death situations that brought this concept clearly into focus. They may be regarded as verging on the miraculous or supernatural, but without doubt they were some of the most significant events in his life.

One of these took place during his visit to Inner Mongolia between February and June of 1924, when he accompanied Deguchi Ōnisaburō, head of the Ōmoto religious sect, to survey a site to establish a holy land that would be the center for all religions, as well as the basis of a new world socio-political order. Conditions were unsettled and violent throughout the region, and the trip was made at the risk of their lives.

We cannot go into details of this adventure, but the group headed for their destination in the Xing'an district accompanied by a band of soldiers known as the Inner and Outer Mongolia Independence Army. They were attacked several times by Chinese Nationalist soldiers and the groups of marauding mounted bandits found throughout the area. In the mountain passes on their approach to Tongliao they were ambushed from all sides. It is said that the Founder believed death was inevitable and prepared himself for the end. But as he faced the hail of bullets, he experienced an imperturbable calmness and, without moving from his position, avoided the oncoming bullets by a slight shifting of the body. Miraculously he escaped not only uninjured but untouched. The Founder later recounted this incident in his own words:

> I couldn't move from where I stood. So when the bullets came flying towards me, I simply twisted my body and turned my head. Soon, when I concentrated my vision, I could intuitively tell from which direction the enemy would fire, aiming from the right or pointing their rifles from the left. I could see pebbles of white light flashing just before the bullets. I avoided them by twisting and turning my body, and they barely missed me. This happened repeatedly with barely time to breathe, but suddenly I had an insight into the essence of budō. I saw clearly that the movements in martial arts come alive when the center of ki is concentrated in one's mind and body and that the calmer I became, the clearer my mind became. I could intuitively see the thoughts, including the violent intentions, of the other. The calm mind is like the quiet center of a spinning top; because of the calm center, the top is able to spin smoothly and rapidly. It almost seems to be standing still. This is the clarity of mind and body [*sumi-kiri*] that I experienced.

A later incident in the Founder's life further convinced him of the clarity attainable by a calm mind and body. This happened one spring day in 1925 at his Ayabe dōjō, when he was challenged by a naval officer armed with a sword. The Founder faced his attacker with only his bare hands. Whenever the opponent lashed out with his weapon, he moved his body ever so slightly and avoided the thrust or slash of the sword. The fluid evasive movements of the Founder were too much for the naval officer, who soon gave up, totally exhausted. Later the Founder recalled this event, saying:

> It was nothing. Just a matter of clarity of mind and body. When the opponent attacked, I could see a flash of white light, the size of a pebble, flying before the sword. I could see clearly that when a white light gleamed, the sword would follow immediately. All I did was avoid the streams of white light.

In this incident, identical with the experience he had had in Inner Mongolia, the Founder was able to perceive, intuitively and instantaneously, even the subtlest movement resulting from an enemy's antagonistic thought. In later years he referred to such subtle perceptions and insights as "the vibrations of the body echoing the vibrations of the universe," and composed such poems as:

Standing amidst heaven and earth
Connected to all things with ki,
My mind is set
On the path of echoing all things.

Such was the realization of the essence or heart of aikidō, and from this developed the Founder's thoughts on love and harmony.

Leading the Opponent

Freedom and spontaneity in spherical movement are characteristic of the techniques basic to aikidō. As far as body movements involving turning and pivoting (*tai-sabaki*) are concerned, spherical motions and movements are the alpha and omega of training. This emphasis on the dynamism of the sphere has led to various interesting developments.

For example, despite the fact that aikidō teaches rough techniques, such as direct strikes (*atemi*) and wrist holds inherited from ancient fighting arts, the emphasis on spherical rotation gives the visual impression of a smoothly flowing choreographed dance, refined and delicate. Furthermore, many techniques create a wide arc, such as throwing an opponent, leading him to the ground or following his movements, yet aikidō can be performed within a limited space. This is due to thc spherical motions of aikidō, in contrast to the linear movements of other martial art forms, where the direct forward or backward thrust gives the appearance of greater violence and requires a much larger area for performance.

In effect, what were originally hard, rough techniques have been smoothed and refined by the emphasis on spherical movement, and techniques requiring a large space became contained in a small sphere. This is probably one reason why aikidō is regarded as a highly sophisticated art.

It should be immediately noted that the spherical movements in aikidō were not developed for the purpose of refining the art or for developing a passive kind of defense. The explicit aim was positive and aggressive: to overcome and control the strength of the opponent. Aikidō was born from the struggle to answer such vital questions as: What would I do when confronted by someone physically stronger than myself? How can I overcome the other without using weapons of any kind? Without resorting to foolhardy violence or psychological trickery while retaining the integrity of budō, what is the most rational form of subduing an opponent? In a word, how can we devise a defense against someone superior in size, strength and experience?

The principle and application of spherical rotation as basic to aikidō was originated by Master Ueshiba in response to such questions and was developed by him as a modern challenge to traditional martial arts. The Founder mastered various forms of jūjutsu, such as the Kitō and Daitō schools, and he trained in the ancient art of swordsmanship of the Shinkage School. Dissatisfied with what he had learned, he underwent rigorous training and discipline and, with the philosophy of nen as the basis, advocated a free and spontaneous manifestation of self in spherical motion.

The principle that the soft controls the hard, the flexible conquers the rigid, found in classical jūjutsu was inherited by Master Ueshiba in his formulation of aikidō, but with a fundamental difference. In ancient jūjutsu they taught that "when pushed, pull back; when pulled, push forward." In the spherical movements of aikidō, this becomes, "when pushed, pivot and go around; when pulled, enter while circling." This means that one moves in circular motion in response to the opponent and while moving spherically, one maintains his center of gravity to create the stable axis of movement. And at the same time the opponent's center is disturbed, and when he loses his center, he also loses all power. Then he is subdued swiftly and decisively.

In the language of aikidō this point is most pertinent to the body movements involving turning and pivoting, known as *tai-sabaki*, whose basic technique is entering or, more precisely, *irimi-issoku*, "entering with a single step," based on the principle of spherical rotation. Standing face to face with an opponent in the *hanmi* stance, when the opponent moves forward, one avoids the linear thrust and enters into the opening outside his vision, which is called *shikaku* or dead angle. The key point here is swift, sure footwork where one's center takes over the opponent's center. The basic technique involves a strike (*atemi*) to the opponent's unprotected, vulnerable spot as one enters, but with advanced training various moves are executed (such as *irimi-nage*, *irimi-tenkan*, *irimi-otoshi*).

As I have noted, irimi is basic to the principle of spherical rotation, and the most important consideration is to always maintain one's center of gravity. From the standpoint of actual engagement it is crucial to enter with the full force of ki to take over the opponent's center and to take charge of the situation. Any hesitation about entering when a direct blow is coming at you is to be avoided at all costs. There are many other important points, but since this work is not meant to be a detailed explanation of techniques, we refer you to manuals devoted to them.

If irimi represents the characteristics of budō as manifested in martial technique, then proper body movement, tai-sabaki, symbolizes the essential features of aikidō expressed through motions that contribute to harmonizing with dynamic change. Ultimately, the techniques of body movement are based on spiritual unity with the order of the cosmos and dynamic unity with the everchanging universe.

Body movement in aikidō is based on the principle of spherical rotation. Just as in the case of a spherical body, the center is stable and movement comes from this still point. This spherical movement can control any counterforce by techniques coming from its center, graceful yet filled with infinite power. We may call on the laws of physics, such as centrifugal and centripetal forces to explain aikidō movements, but their essential beauty comes from the unity of ki-mind-body. Because it is an experience of an integrated, whole person, objective analysis does not really add to our understanding, let alone mastery, of it.

The aikidō student must devote the major part of his training to mastering the techniques of spherical rotation, and through constant training study the basic principle involved. In movement he or she becomes like a spinning top, stable in the center, never losing balance. Even though the student may not be fully aware of it, the unity of ki-mind-body which is one with the universe has been achieved.

The character for *ki* written in the calligraphy of Master Ueshiba Morihei.

The Founder in his later years (1968) gives a demonstration with the staff showing the mysterious combination of *ki-shin-tai* (ki-mind-body) in technique.

Around 1960.

The Founder performing the *kokyū-nage* technique. (1956)

At the Aiki Shrine, Iwama Ibaraki Prefecture. (1962)

Irimi-nage technique. (1968)

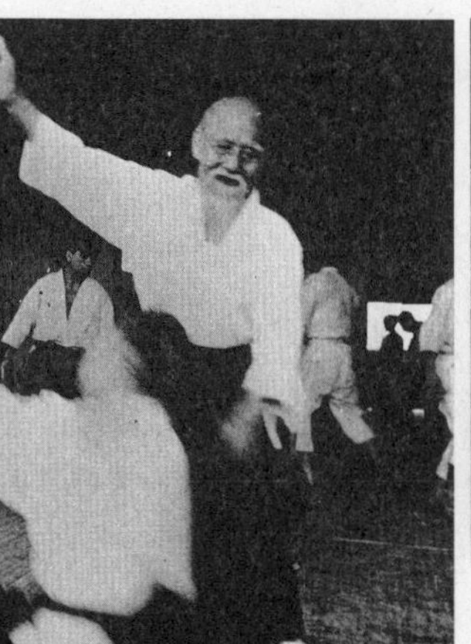

Using a folding fan to control a sword attack from the front.

The Dōshu receives personal instruction from the Founder. (*ca*. 1955)

The Founder and the Dōshu talk of aikidō's past and future in a discussion that lasts deep into the night. (*ca*. 1955)

The Dōshu during a recent demonstration at the Iwama Aiki Shrine Festival. (1984)

The ki flows as the Dōshu exercises in the early morning light among the cryptomeria at Kumano Shrine in Wakayama Prefecture. (1982)

Delegates at the general meeting of the International Aikidō Federation held in Paris in 1980.

The Dōshu gives a demonstration in Los Angeles during a trip to the United States. (1982)

The Dōshu visited the New York Aikikai on the occasion of its twentieth anniversary. (1984)

The Dōshu lectures during a recent trip to Australia. (Sydney, 1984)

Master Ueshiba Morihei, Founder of Aikidō.

Daily Practice, the Way to Perfection

Young Practitioners and Aikidō Basics

In recent years, the increase in the number of young students of aikidō has been dramatic. At the Hombu Dōjō alone there are more than 500 students ranging from first graders to junior high school students, and dōjō throughout the country report a similar phenomenon, a number of them registering more than a hundred students. The annual summer Aikidō Youth Training Conference held at the Nippon Budōkan and the summer and winter camps sponsored by the Hombu Dōjō at Sugadaira in Nagano Prefecture and Izu in Shizuoka Prefecture are well attended and the enthusiasm is truly contagious.

The question of starting a children's class at the Hombu Dōjō first arose almost twenty years ago. The reason for debating the feasibility of such a move was that aikidō stresses not only physical movements, but sooner or later requires understanding the philosophy behind it. Sportslike or gamelike elements that would hold the interest of young children are minimal, and we had to seriously deliberate our decision. To our great surprise and satisfaction the majority of students have continued aikidō practice down through the years. In the end, one could not help being impressed by the sincerity and earnestness shown in practice by younger people. These are most assuredly essential qualities for any aikidō student, beginner or advanced. This is a point we must never forget.

Some time ago an assistant Hombu Dōjō instructor who taught a children's class at a branch dōjō expressed amazement at their rapid progress. He was impressed by their intense curiosity, openness and willingness to repeatedly practice the same movements. He also found they were very perceptive and could read the teacher's mind by the way he spoke, chose his words, or looked at them. In fact, unless the teacher was sincere in scolding or praising the students, they would not respect him. This instructor had been training for fifteen years, but on this occasion he learned from the children that the spirit of harmony and true love are essential for teaching aikidō. And he added that while teaching the basics of aikidō to the children, he was taught the basics of love and harmony by them. The curiosity and desire of children for aikidō are far beyond the imagination of most adults.

The training method for children and youth differs from that for adults but the basics and the progression are essentially the same. As in adult classes, the students begin with the preliminaries, such as the *funakogi* (boat rowing) and *furitama* (ki settling) exercises. These were devised by the Founder, when he realized that "this self is none other than the universe," as methods of inviting the divine essence into one's own center.

In the boat-rowing exercise, one stands with one leg forward and the other back, clenching both hands as if they held oars. The hips become the center of a repetitious forward and backward movement that resembles rowing. Throughout the back and forth movements, ki is maintained in the centrum as a method of unifying mind and body. The students truly enjoy the rhythmic movements in spite of the peculiar name and the motions involved.

After these preliminaries students are taught to fall by rolling forward and backward and eventually practice being lead by the spherical movement of a partner. This is known as the practice of *ukemi*, the one who leads being known as the *nage* and the one who is lead or thrown as the *uke*. Next, they proceed to seated movements and floor techniques called *shikko* and *suwari-waza*. Since the Japanese people are rapidly losing the custom of sitting formal style on tatami, I feared that children may rebel or find it difficult to perform them, but this proved not to be so, and to my delight they really enjoyed working out on the floor.

These floor exercises are based on *seiza*, the formal style of sitting. Once this becomes a natural sitting posture, as required at the beginning and end of each aikidō class, it leads by itself to the development of proper etiquette.

From ancient times one dictum of budō has been: "Begin with etiquette, conclude with etiquette." The etiquette taught in aikidō—mutual respect, consideration for others, cleanliness—is not forced upon students by indoctrination or threats. It is the natural consequence of learning to sit properly in seiza and mastering the basics of suwari-waza. The upright body is related to the upright mind. The crux of the matter lies in respect for the individual student, who out of his center and initiative will want to behave in accordance with the highest standards of conduct. Etiquette is an important aspect of practice for all aikidō students.

The seiza sitting posture, a civilized, formal custom among the Japanese since ancient times, is the source of natural etiquette imprinted in people's minds. Even though the custom of seiza may be on the wane in daily life, it is my conviction that its spiritual and ethical roots will not easily disappear. And when I see children in the dōjō sitting in seiza with their backs upright and both hands placed on their folded knees, I feel again that it must continue to have a central place in aikidō training. It is the source of proper etiquette, it is basic to many techniques, and it is essential for good training.

After personally observing aikidō practice among children and young people, I came to the conclusion that the decision to hold classes for them was justified. At the same time I feel a sense of responsibility lest we neglect to transmit the moral and spiritual essence of aikidō to them. Especially is this true when juvenile delinquency is becoming a world-wide problem. The blame for this problem cannot be simply placed on the young; we adults must also bear responsibility.

Earlier, I pointed out that some people have a misconception of what aikidō is. Now I must note that there are people who misunderstand the purpose of aikidō. Especially among parents whose children are not as aggressive or as strong as others, there is a tendency to push them into aikidō as if it were the answer to their problem. To think that aikidō will make their children tougher and stronger does injustice both to their children and to aikidō. Aikidō rejects all forms of violence, justified or unjustified. Otherwise, we would be no different from the forms of martial arts in which fighting and winning are selling points.

At the risk of seeming repetitious, I want to say again that aikidō is a spiritual path and its ideal is the realization of harmony and love. By disciplining mind and body, especially mind, it leads to the perfection of personality and humanity. What we teach children is not brute force, not violence, but the cultivation of ki through mind-body training which will eventually build confidence, self-esteem and a sense of control over their lives.

We thus seek to have both children and parents understand clearly the purpose of aikidō. The instructor, too, must keep the central purpose of our art always in mind, and when teaching children, never think that they are incapable of grasping the fundamentals of aikidō. Children, too, should be regarded as individuals who seek to grow on the path of love and harmony as does each of us regardless of age.

Expanding the Circle of Aikidō

Along with the importance of training for children and youth, another characteristic of aikidō that differentiates it from other martial arts is the great number of women students.

Even in Japan in recent years, the number of women in almost all forms of sports, except for boxing and sumo, has been on the increase. In the martial arts, women are active in judo, kendo, karate, kenpo and so on, but it seems that aikidō has attracted a proportionately greater number of women. This phenomenon has not been purely a matter of numbers. It has been qualitative as well, in that women's training adds depth and breadth to aikidō.

There is considerable variety in motivation and reasons for practicing aikidō, and there are women of all ages and professions who are dedicated to the path, remain with it for many years, and seek the highest spiritual ideals of budō. In a sense, it seems that aikidō is open especially to women so that they can easily enter its gates and naturally become part of its process of self-development.

Is this the reason aikidō is sometimes misconstrued in very strange ways? Many are the simplistic questions and statements about it. People ask, "Is aikidō a martial art for women?" They say, "It seems to favor women." Or even, "It's effeminate." Some remarks are sexist, such as "Isn't mixed practice distracting?" Or "Don't so many women get in the way of real practice?" Other questions seem to arise naturally. "Women aren't interested in budo. Don't they think of aikidō only as a form of self-defense, or just exercise for health and beauty?" "Aren't women treated with diffidence, given special treatment?"

Again, the questions and criticism arise from ignorance about aikidō.

If a person had done even a minimal amount of aikidō training, knew something of its philosophy, and realized the rigorous discipline required to attain its highest goal, he would never make such comments.

Simply stated, aikidō is a budō open to all people who aspire to unify the ki of the universe with the ki of oneself. For all members of the human race, it is the path to attaining harmony with all beings. The gates of aikidō are open to people of all ages, classes, sexes, nationalities and races. Non-discrimination and non-exclusiveness are basic characteristics of aikidō. As in the case of young people and of the older practitioners to be discussed later, women are not objects of any kind of discrimination. Moreover, to accuse aikidō of favoring women or giving them preferential treatment, simply because of their comparatively high number, is to be guilty of latent sexism.

While aikidō favors neither women nor men, it is true that traditional budō, developed in an age of feudalism, was regarded as an exclusively male domain. Criticism of aikidō as being effeminate or favoring women is nothing but a remnant of this outdated attitude. Since this is a serious problem that pertains to the present and future of the martial arts, we should examine such attitudes more carefully.

The ancient fighting arts originated in an age when only men faced life or death on the battlefield, and the view that budō was a special male domain may have once been justified. In our modern world, when martial arts should be the training of both mind and body, this view is completely anachronistic. The idea that martial arts should be confined to men rested on the assumption of violence and brute force, but this is no longer a valid assumption. Modern budō as the way of mind-body training is based on the assumption of love and harmony. Aikidō is the foremost budō that seeks to cultivate true humanity in a peaceful world.

Aikidō for women is clearly budō, and there is no difference in the training of women and men. Women who actually undergo aikidō practice come to know this. This is not to deny that some women do enter aikidō thinking it is useful for self-defense, or an ideal exercise for health and beauty. They have been misled by newspaper and magazine articles describing the popularity of aikidō among women, which reflect the prejudices we have just discussed.

Once they begin training, they realize that aikidō means repeated practice, requiring unity of mind and body and the cultivation of ki-power. That it may be beneficial to health and beauty or as self-defense is purely a by-product unrelated to the spirit of aikidō. To seek such results quickly and as an end in themselves will undermine the true appreciation of what aikidō has to offer.

Some women (as well as men) may feel resistance to the repetitious practice of basic postures, but this is a necessary preliminary to learning techniques. Learning proper distancing (ma-ai) in facing an opponent may prove unexpectedly difficult, as may performing footwork movements in a smooth, sliding manner, as found in Noh dance. The cultivation of breath-power or ki, originating in the centrum and extending through the arms and hands, may initially pose a problem for others. The mastery of ukemi, taking falls, while always maintaining one's center and balance may have to be practiced over and over again. The difficulties encountered by beginners, including confusion, perspiration and occasional bruises, do not seem to deter them. According to them, the difficulties are a challenge rather than a discouragement and actually strengthen the motivation to master aikidō.

Men make similar comments, but it seems that women generally have more stamina, patience and the will to continue on the path, and this is probably related to unconscious creative powers that they possess. Women who enter the gates of aikidō rarely leave training soon after they begin. At least eight out of ten continue, and the longer and deeper they study, the more they become enraptured with aikidō. The reason for this is not always clear, but a general idea may be gleaned from comments made in interviews in newspapers and magazines and in essays appearing from time to time in the newsletters published by the Hombu Dōjō.

> "I couldn't even do a somersault when I began aikidō, so when I took my first forward roll, I felt like my day was made."
>
> "Within half a year my body became as light as a ball when I was thrown. I think aikidō made me stronger as a person, and although I have no particular thoughts on budō, I do think I'm learning to appreciate it."
>
> "Because of constant seiza practice, my posture has really improved. My teachers in tea ceremony and flower arranging often

mention it, and my Japanese dance teacher says my foot movement and stance have become very good."

"When I practiced judo, I always had an inferiority complex because of the men, who were stronger, and I didn't like some of the floor techniques. But with aikidō, since the aim is not the display of mere strength and none of the techniques are offensive, I really enjoy it."

"I really like being an uke, because when I'm thrown, all my pride and vanity disappear. Aikidō has been called 'dynamic Zen.' When I'm able to become myself openly through practice, I really think it might be something like Zen."

"One reason I continue at the dōjō is because of the harmonious atmosphere. I get to practice with various kinds of people, and there is no rivalry, because no one wins or loses. This has affected my own attitude to others. I try to work with others and listen more carefully to what they have to say."

"As I began to master the principle of spherical movement, my ability to handle my daily chores improved. I don't waste time any more, and my world has become richer and fuller. Aikidō is a necessary part of my life. Now I couldn't live without it."

Comments like these come from college teachers, office workers, housewives, students, doctors, secretaries and others of various ages and callings. Despite the differences, I sense a common theme. They have all grasped, more or less, the essence of aikidō intuitively and experientially, and their comments, differing from those made by men, are more closely related to daily living. This means that, while there is no discrimination between men and women in the contents and practice of aikidō, a natural distinction appears in their responses to it. This is good for aikidō because it breaks the stereotypes people have about martial arts.

In aikidō the individuality of each person is respected, and the strength of each individual is developed and nurtured. While the training and philosophy of aikidō have universal application, each response, whether from man or woman, depends on the individual. Aikidō is neither masculine nor feminine, nor should there be any prior assumption about how men or women should act or perform in aikidō.

Another recent phenomenon in aikidō is the increase in the number of families becoming involved in practice. As noted previously, many parents encourage their children to take up aikidō. Then, as they regularly visit the dōjō, they themselves become interested and begin to practice. This is especially true of parents and grandparents who experienced aikidō in their youth and who are now encouraging their children and grandchildren. An amazing number of mothers who bring their children to practice have also become regular aikidō practitioners.

The worldwide aikidō population, as of 1981, of members belonging to the main tradition of Master Ueshiba (known officially as the Aikikai and including the Hombu Dōjō; more than 250 branch dōjō in Japan; university, company, and government office clubs; and overseas dōjō) numbers more than 500,000 in Japan and more than 100,000 abroad, for a total approaching 700,000. If the aikidō schools begun by the Founder's original students, their subschools and groups that are aikidō in name only are added to this, the total number is even greater.

The Continuity of Tradition

Having discussed the significant place and role of younger students and women practitioners, I do not want to close this chapter without mentioning the countless people in the past who have preserved the continuity of aikidō tradition. Their contributions appear especially significant in the light of the Fiftieth Anniversary Celebration in October, 1981, of the founding of the headquarters dōjō at the present site of the Aikidō Hombu Dōjō in Tokyo.

It was in 1931 that the Founder, then forty-eight years old, established the permanent headquarters of aikidō, an art he had been gradually formulating during the 1920s. This first 80-tatami Hombu Dōjō was at the same location in Tokyo as the present headquarters. Now fifty years have elapsed. For a person who grew up with the Founder as both teacher and father, fifty years seem such a short time, yet it is a very long time. At other times, I think a half century is such a long time, yet so very, very short.

His achievements fill my heart with pride and satisfaction, but I also want to remember and pay my respects to all the fellow practitioners and supporters of the art during the past fifty to sixty years, who contributed to the growth of aikidō but are no longer with us. My gratitude goes, too, to all those who have been associated with aikidō since before World War II and who still continue to advise, encourage, and support us in every way possible.

Among the people I remember are those who lived in the same household as the Founder as *uchideshi*, or direct disciples, and received his guidance on the personal as well as the professional level. There were many other students who were not *uchideshi* but nevertheless studied with Master Ueshiba and were completely dedicated to the way of aikidō. Nor should we forget the leaders in society who out of deep respect and affection for the Founder gave him martial and moral support to develop his new budō. And there are many others to whom we are indebted for their roles in maintaining and helping with the spread of aikidō. These include people with whom I spent many years in training under the Founder, those who pioneered in establishing dōjō throughout Japan and abroad, and those who, after the Founder's death, offered their kind assistance in carrying on the tradition. Space does not permit me to acknowledge each by name, but as I recall their names and faces, the half century of aikidō history passes through my mind as if it had occurred only yesterday.

Certain highlights in that history stand out. There was "Hell Dōjō," a nickname used because of strong and powerful students, each an individual in his own right, who gathered around the Founder's training hall. . . . The Founder's passion to spread aikidō that lead him to his adventures in Inner Mongolia. . . . The period of his retirement to Iwama, where the Aiki Shrine is located, and where he aspired to unite the goals of aikidō with a life of farming. . . . The years immediately following World War II when aikidō, along with the other martial arts, was proscribed by law, and a handful of his disciples gathered around him and vowed to keep the flames of aikidō burning. . . . Then, on February 9, 1948, the joy of official government approval to establish the Aikikai as a non-profit organization, which began a new chapter in our history.

To recall these events and personalities is to remember moments of dejection and celebration, of sadness and joy. But my wish is that they not remain merely a personal reminiscence, inaccessible to the aikidō practitioners who today enjoy the benefits of the past. We must never forget the contributions, the sacrifices and dedication of the men and women who made aikidō what it is today. One of our tasks is to transmit to later generations the evolutionary phases of aikidō: the period of the founding, of development, of turmoil, of retreat and the period of a new beginning.

As long as such recollections are kept alive, they will remind us that aikidō did not suddenly appear from nowhere. It is the product of a long chain of events, beginning with the Founder and his original disciples whose legacy has been inherited by those who practice aikidō today. Looking back over more than half a century we see members from the second, third and even fourth generations taking up aikidō. Indeed, we have become a large extended family working together for the same goal and having Master Ueshiba as its ancestral head.

Fortunately, many aikidō students are fully aware of our rich heritage, and there is no need for me to remind them. This is quite evident when I see groups of students gathered around instructors as they recount stories about the Founder, based on direct or indirect knowledge. In an atmosphere of conviviality, the history of aikidō is being transmitted naturally and spontaneously to the younger generations. In daily practice, between sessions of rigorous training, such dialogues inspire camaraderie and friendship. This may be a characteristic unique to aikidō, but unconsciously the kind of exchange the Founder enjoyed having with his students is being reenacted, and the effect is to cultivate a sense of history.

Aikidō has been referred to as the budō that brings together young and old, the youthful and the mature. Transcending differences in age and sex, children, adults, men and women practice and encourage each other in training. This makes a striking contrast to those budō in which young, strong, macho types seem to predominate. This is partially due to the fact that aikidō downgrades all forms of competitive tournaments where physical strength is all important and at the same time strives for well-rounded training of both mind and body. Each age group practicing aikidō has its respective ways of achieving the unity of ki-mind-body, but they can all mingle and learn from each other.

In a training atmosphere devoid of age or sex distinctions, mutual respect and communication grow. The children aspire to reach the level of youths, the youths emulate the mastery of ki of the adults, and the adults respect the perspective and flowing movements of the elders. The reverse is also true. The elders are stimulated by the vigor of the young adults, the young adults absorb the energy of the youths, and the youths are reminded of the beginner's mind of the children with its openness and intensity. Out of such a circular interchange grows the power born of harmonious activity, and it also leads to a sense of propriety and etiquette based on mutual respect.

In conclusion, we can say that aikidō seems to have a depth and breadth rarely seen in budō. This cannot but be the result of the emphasis on love and harmony stressed by the Founder throughout his lifetime. Our task, then, is to dedicate ourselves to constant daily practice, always keeping in mind the centrality of love and harmony.

Hikari ("light") in the Founder's calligraphy.

The Founder often used the expression "faster than light" when describing the theory of aikidō. By this he meant that, as the basis of aikidō techniques lies in absorbing the partner's movements into one's own, aikidō is in a spiritual sense faster than a bullet, faster even than light itself. The truly unique feature of aikidō is that one is united with nature, moving with spirit and technique united as one, always in accordance with the principle of spherical rotation.

The movements of aikidō are extremely varied. Rather than following fixed forms, techniques are derived one after the other from a single basic principle. For this reason new techniques are still being born even now. Infinite possibility hidden within the everyday—this is the distinguishing characteristic of aikidō.

The heart of aikidō is perhaps most clearly expressed in *irimi-nage* (entering throw), and in the following pages I use this technique as an example. In contrast with more intricate techniques, the vertical movements at the beginning and lateral movements at the end are most clearly evident.

Irimi-nage is a technique where the *nage* (the one who leads) enters his partner's dead angle (*shikaku*), takes control of his fate, leading and throwing him according to the principle of spherical rotation. One draws the opponent into one's own movement so that the two bodies become as one, then destroys his balance and throws him while keeping him in one's circle of control.

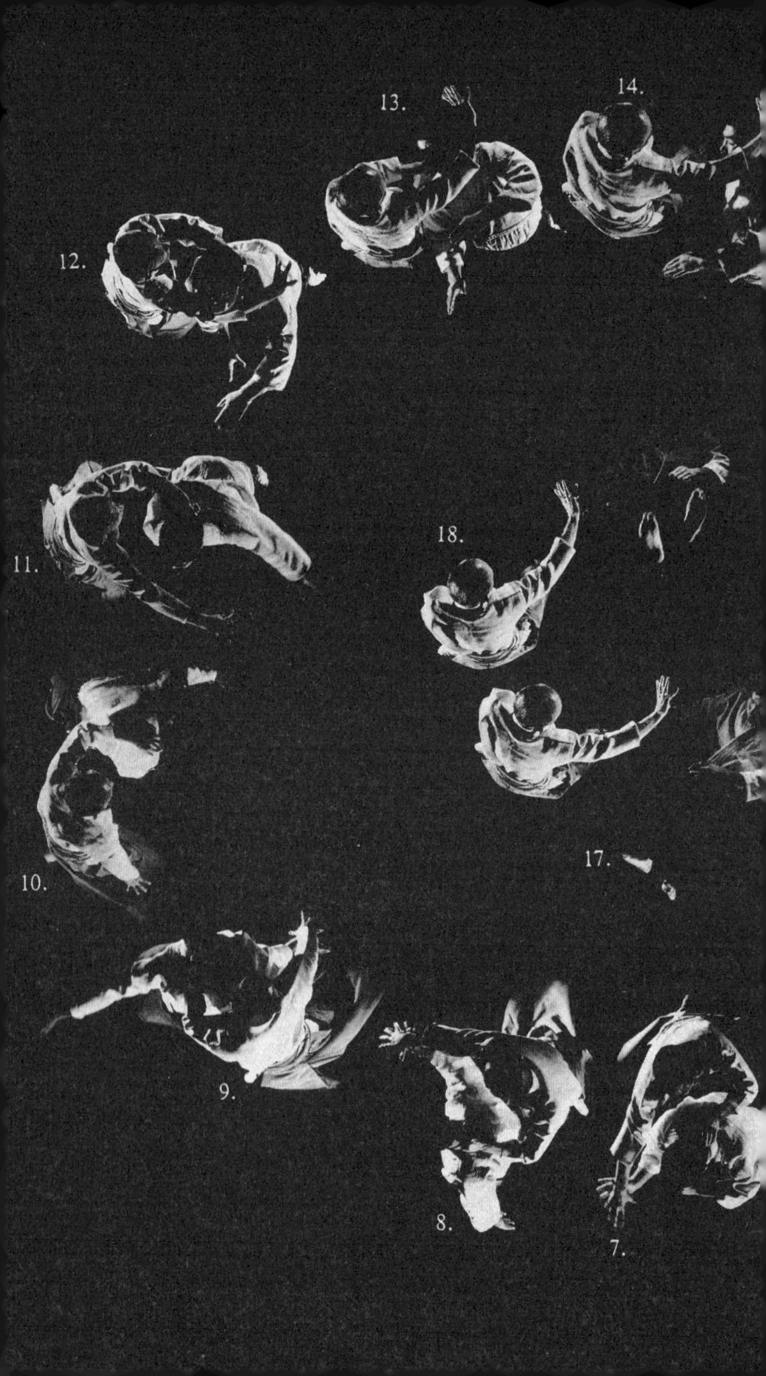
13.
14.
12.
11.
18.
10.
17.
9.
8.
7.

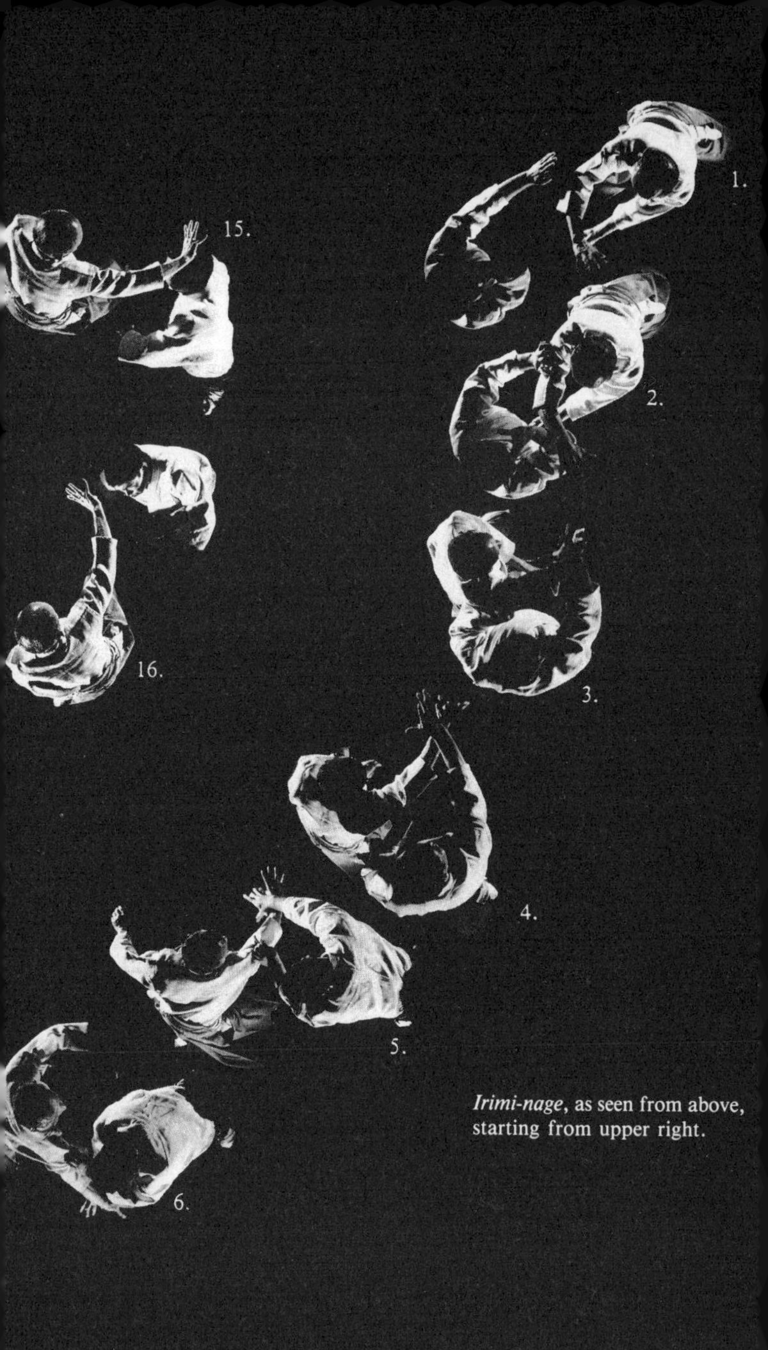

Irimi-nage, as seen from above, starting from upper right.

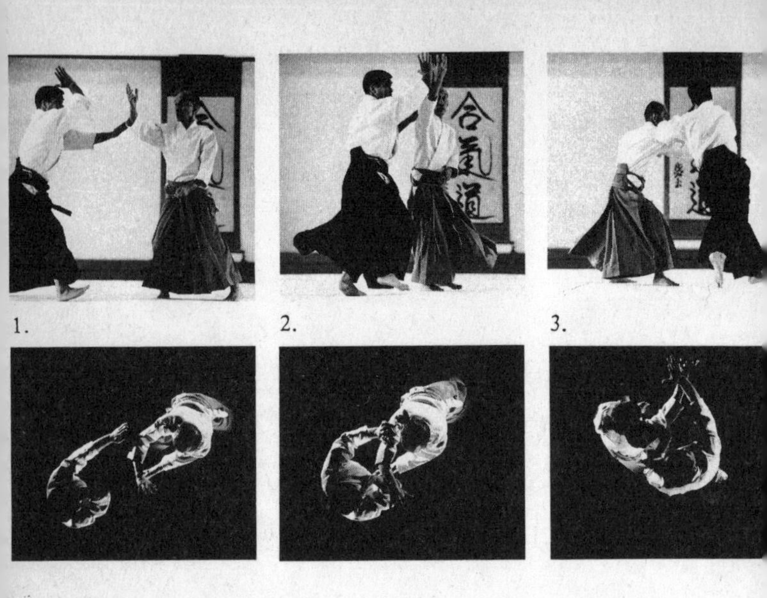

1. 2. 3.

1. Taking the *hanmi* stance, the right sword-hand is extended straight to the partner's front. Drawn by the extended hand, the partner then begins to move to deliver a strike to the chest with his right hand.
The *hanmi* (oblique facing) stance is characteristic of aikidō; one should always move from *hanmi* to *hanmi*.
The basic method of moving the feet in aikidō is called *suri-ashi* (sliding feet). This is the most efficient way of moving while maintaining maximum stability of the hips. When moving in *suri-ashi* it is important for the knees to be flexible yet still give firm support.

2. The partner's right sword-hand comes down as if to cover the nage's. This makes it possible to grab the partner's right shoulder. At this point, the opponent is drawn into the nage's rotational movement.

3. While turning to the left using the right foot as pivot, the opponent is completely enveloped as the two bodies merge together into a single movement.

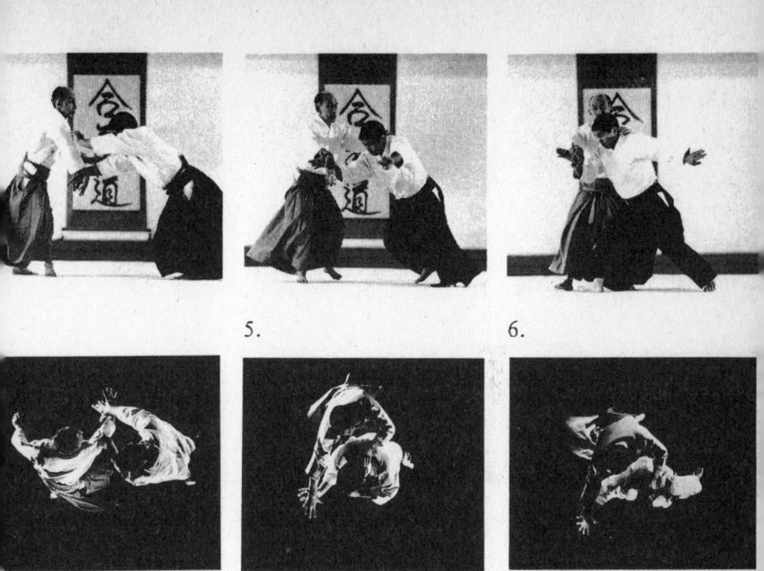

5.

6.

4. This is the point at which the reverse turn occurs. Having pivoted on the right foot, the nage turns 180° to the left, causing his partner to follow the right sword-hand. Seizing this opportunity, the nage then begins the turn to the right, again on the right pivot foot. This free spherical rotation is the essence of aikidō.

5. With the opponent's balance completely destroyed, the two continue to move as one within a single rotational movement. At this time the right sword-hand controls the opponent's wrist, using the strength eminating from the circle's central axis (the center line of the nage's body).

6. Still controlling the opponent, whose direction has now been completely reversed, the nage continues his turn, this time on the left pivot foot.

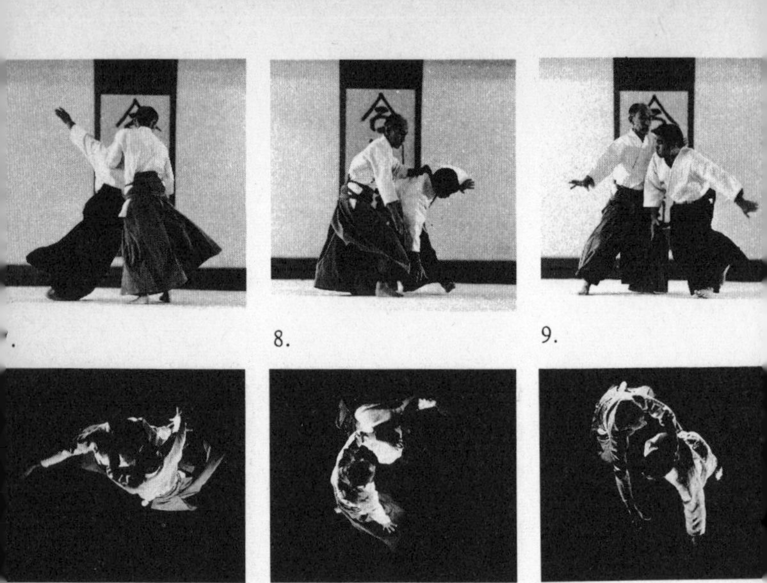

7–9. The turn continues, two bodies as one.

10. With the opponent's balance now broken to the front, the nage seizes on his reflexive inclination to stand up and controls him from above with his right sword-hand. It is imperative that one's own movements be united with the opponent's, as if the two are one body. In other words, the attacker is manipulated as if he were a part of oneself, in a natural way as if he has been absorbed within one's own nature.

11–12. Posture completely broken, the opponent is then felled.

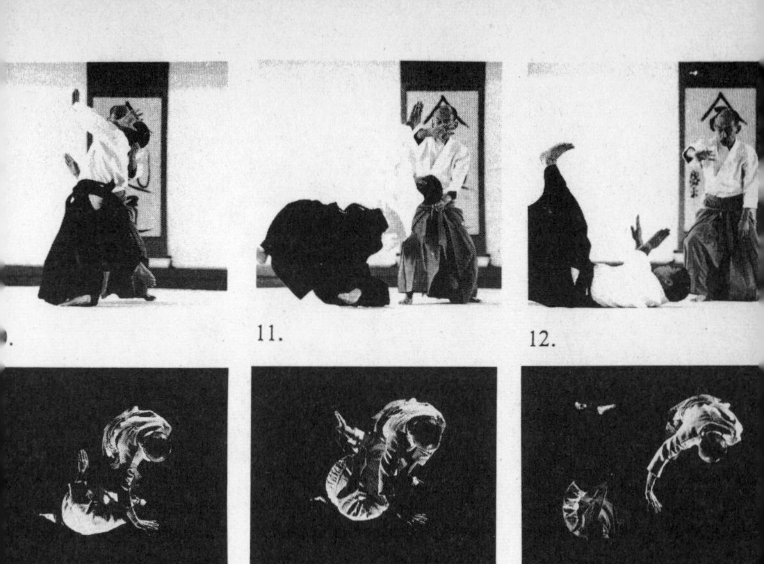

The Dōshu during a demonstration.

Mastering Mind, Cultivating Technique

Ultimate Mastery: Realizing the Heart of Aikidō

Before World War II, a famous German scientist involved in military research came to Japan. When he returned to Germany, he took with him several Japanese swords and entrusted them for scientific analysis to an institute specializing in research and development of high technology steel. The scientist was an admirer of Japanese swords, held them in the highest respect, and knew of their superiority when compared with European swords.

The stark simplicity of the Japanese sword belies its many fine qualities: the extraordinary attention paid to details on the blade and hilt, the sharp, clear feeling of the cut, the soft touch in the hands as the shock of contact is naturally dissipated and the rarity of damage to the hardened cutting edge, the whole being made resilient by a core of softer steel.

He was aware of these qualities, but something bothered him: the air of mysticism that enshrouded the traditional method of forging the steel blade, for the swordsmith, dressed all in white to symbolize purification, does his work before a Shintō altar. This seemed to him very, very primitive, and he also had a low opinion of the sacred awe with which the Japanese regard the sword. He wanted to penetrate the mystery and unravel the secrets, but no matter how earnestly he requested it, he was never permitted to watch the swordsmith at work.

Thus it was that he decided to have a scientific analysis made of the materials and the method of production. With the scientific data gathered in the laboratory at hand , he thought he would reconstruct the sword using the most recent technology available at the time. As a German with absolute confidence in the efficacy of science, he must have been convinced that an exact replica of the Japanese sword could be manufactured, and he may have imagined that he could show up the old-fashioned, esoteric techniques of the swordsmith.

The outcome was utter failure. Collecting scientific data posed no problem, of course, but when he actually tried to make a sword, the result was just another commonplace sword. His use of scientific know-how, even with repeated experimentation and modification of the production method, ended in disappointment. Finally, he was forced to give up his attempt and acknowledge the superiority of the "old-fashioned, esoteric" method of Japanese swordmaking.

This episode suggests that even though traditional Japanese craftsmanship can be subjected to modern, scientific analysis, there will always remain an element or ingredient that escapes conventional scrutiny or analysis. In traditional technology much of the achievement is due to an intuitive quality, known as the working of *kan*, and this can be acquired only through the accumulation of years of training. For *kan*-intuition to work, one must experience a creative tension stemming from single-minded concentration on the work in progress. This opens the way for a higher power, *kami* in Japanese, to enter into the process. Much of the success depends on becoming filled with divine consciousness or *kami*. The Japanese craftsman in making a single sword relies on kan both to select the proper materials and to combine them in the precise way transmitted in his family. It is not too much to say that the entire process of firing, forging and cooling is dependent on the elusive working of kan.

If we think of the Japanese sword in terms of the blade and the hilt, the blade consists of the sharp edge of the sword, the tip, the back of the blade and the *shinogi* (a lengthwise ridge between the edge of the sword and its back). Each of the parts has a slightly different function in sword fighting, and accordingly each is made with different materials and methods. These subtle differences are all determined by kan-intuition born out of intense concentration and an almost religious devotion to the craft. This is why the swordsmith has an altar enshrining kami in his workplace, wears ceremonial white garments, and performs purification rites as an integral part of the swordmaking process. In this solemn atmosphere, he can let his mind become settled; then he is ready to begin his task.

To the swordsmith, his work is a sacred art, for unless this be so, the kami will become irritated and upset his kan-intuition. Not only the parts, but the Japanese sword as a whole, are born from intuition and divine power, both of which may be beyond scientific analysis and hence "mysterious." That the German scientist, attracted by the mystic beauty of the Japanese sword, attempted a scientific analysis was in itself a contradiction, and it was only natural that his experiment should fail.

Similarly, we have difficulty in trying to explain the *ultimate essence* of aikidō when asked by a novice or an outsider. The words defy simple verbal explication. The ultimate essence is an individual, intuitive experience of people who by good fortune may come to realize it after years of training and seeking. A composite of complex factors, it is part of the wisdom contained in traditional Japanese artistic achievement. Its nature is such that as long as one strives on the path of training with the goal of achieving it, the realization will come sooner or later. This kind of trust, together with nen-insight, will unlock the heart of aikidō and bring the ultimate essence into realization.

Being highly individualistic, although available universally, this essence will be realized differently, depending on the person and his or her level of attainment. This is the reason that a general statement cannot be made without creating some misunderstanding. Nevertheless, it is clear that the ultimate essence is the highest realization attained by the Founder in his years of relentless training and quest. We will, therefore, turn to some sayings which reveal his understanding of the essence. These should be carefully digested, since, depending on the stage of training, they may for a particular person be but tentative expressions of the ultimate realization.

> I undertook the training of my body through budō, and when I realized its ultimate essence, I gained an even higher truth. When I realized the core of universal reality, I saw clearly that human beings must unify mind and body and the ki that connects the two and that a person must harmonize his activity with the activity of all things in the universe. Through the subtle working of ki, mind and body are harmonized and the relationship between the individual and the universe is harmonized.
>
> If the subtle working of ki is not properly utilized, a person's

mind and body will become unhealthy, the world will become chaotic, and the entire universe will be thrown into disorder. Aikidō is the way of truth. Training in aikidō is training in truth. Through dedication, training and penetration, divine performance will be born.

Only by pursuing the following three types of training will the immovable truth of diamondlike hardness become part of one's mind and body.

1. Training to harmonize one's mind with the activity of all things in the universe.
2. Training to harmonize one's body with the activity of all things in the universe.
3. Training to make the ki that connects mind and body harmonize with the activity of all things in the universe.

The true student of aikidō is one who practices and realizes these three points simultaneously, not merely theoretically but actually, in the dōjō and at every moment in daily life.

Master Ueshiba repeatedly taught:

Every technique of a martial art must be in accord with the truth of the universe. If it is not, the martial art will be isolated and go against the love-creating martial art of *take-musu* [literally, martial-creative]. Aikidō is *take-musu* par excellence. Martial [*take*] here means the heroic roar, the resonance of the body, the power of *aum* that resounds in the universe.

The resonance of the body derives from the unity of mind and body which harmonizes with the resonance of the universe. The mutual response and interchange produce the ki of ai-ki. The essence of aikidō is the mutual echoing of the resonance of the body with the resonance of the universe. From this appear heat, light and power united in a fully realized spirit. The vitality of echoing of the body and the resonance of the universe nurture the subtle working of ki and give birth to *take-musu* ai-ki, the martial art that is love and love that is none other than martial art.

To the question of how one achieves the unity of the ki of the universe with the ki of the self, their harmonious working and mutual response, the answer is through intensive training and practice. This makes harmony and love the essence of aikidō. Both are at the heart of aikidō. The Founder considered this to be the ultimate essence and the highest truth.

For the average practitioner such a philosophical approach may seem beyond comprehension. He may then seek a more practical example of the essence as manifested in actual movement and technique. And in fact the Founder disliked teaching by words and preferred that each person realize it through training and practice, as expressed in his poem:

Ai-ki cannot be exhausted
By words written or spoken.
Without dabbling in idle talk,
Understand through practice.

This is identical to the realization that it is impossible to know the secret of the Japanese sword by analysis. It can be known personally only through actual experience. All matters related to the human heart and spirit are of such a nature.

When Master Ueshiba did explain the essence and truth of aikidō in more practical terms, it was usually through poetry or occasional lectures to his disciples. Their number is by no means small, and since each reflects only an aspect of his philosophy, they may be open to misinterpretation and therefore should be treated with care. But for the benefit of those who may be interested in a sampling of his poems and lectures a few are given below.

Among his poems the following may be instructive:

Attacking with a long sword,
The enemy thinks I'm in front of him.
Ah, behind him.
I'm already standing there.

Even though surrounded
By several enemies set to attack,
Fight with the thought
That they are but one.

When entering a forest of spears
And they encircle you,
Remember, your mind
Is your protective shield.

With your right hand
Showing yang,
Your left hand showing yin,
Lead your opponent.

When the enemy comes
Running to strike you,
Step aside, avoid him,
Immediately attack, and cut.

Why do you fix your eyes
On the swinging sword?
His grip reveals
Where he wants to cut.

These poems, written early in his career when the Founder was at the height of his powers, express the ultimate essence of aikidō on the field of life-or-death combat. In later years he avoided the use of the word *enemy*, but the gist of the art to be practiced in the dōjō is nevertheless clear. The brief hints regarding the essence of aikidō as seen in these poems should be evident to regular practitioners. References are made to entering, spherical rotation, sword-hand, direct strike and the confrontation of one against many. The crucial point is the attitude of the mind. Let us cite a few passages from the lectures recorded by the Founder's disciples on various occasions.

> Don't simply look at the opponent's eyes, because they will absorb your mind. Don't just look at the opponent's sword, because it will take away your ki. Don't just look at your opponent, because his ki will control you. Martial arts training is the training of the magnetic power in yourself to absorb the other as he is. That's why all I need to do is to just stand here.

> Don't get caught up in technical discussions about striking before the opponent. Doing so is proof that you're too conscious of the other. In aikidō there is an opponent, but in reality there is no opponent. Because the other is one with self, if one moves as one desires, the other also moves as one desires. So, if one moves as one wishes, the other will naturally comply.

> Anyone should be able to hold down another person with one finger. Human strength is confined to a circle with the individual at the center. Strength can't go beyond that circle. No matter how strong a man is, once he is extended beyond his circle, he has no power. If one tries to hold another down outside his circle of power, then, since he is powerless, he himself can be held down even with the little finger. If one can move within his own circle of power and force the other outside his own circle, then the matter is already decided.

> True breathing means to breath in unison with the universe. Then one gains the power of nature. Spiraling rightwards, he ascends. Spiraling leftwards, he descends. One spirals and rotates freely in heaven and earth. The crucial point is to fully realize the principle of breathing-spiraling.

These passing comments made by the Founder contain the essence of aikidō. Easy to talk about, they are immensely difficult to realize in practice. And we must never forget that the Founder himself came to a philosophical interpretation only after years of rigorous practice and discipline.

Although it is extremely difficult to demonstrate the ultimate essence of aikidō practically, we may attempt this by turning our attention to a basic technique, *shihō-nage* or the four-direction throw. It may not be possible to discuss this fully and convincingly on the printed page, but our purpose here is to understand the underlying principle of this technique, which is inherently one with certain movements in the art of swordsmanship. Aikidō students, of course, know that many other basic waza have close affinities with the use of the sword.

Applying the Principle of Swordsmanship

The Way of aiki and the Way of the sword are intimately connected in basic principles, movements and methods. On the surface the two appear to be radically different, because aikidō is an empty-handed martial art, whereas the art of swordsmanship makes use of a weapon. But once the surface is penetrated many points in common will be noted. (The reference here is to *kenjutsu*, combative swordsmanship, rather then to kendo, which is a modern sport. The similarity to aikidō is found not so much in kendo as in its predecessor.)

A common assumption is that aikidō is more closely related to judo then to swordsmanship. This is understandable because both are empty-handed forms of martial art, and if one knows even a little about the Founder's background, he will be aware of the major formative role played by jūjutsu in the development of aikidō. The Founder, trained in the Daitō school of jūjutsu, incorporated some of its methods into aikidō, and such techniques as the wrist-lock, strikes, throws and pins have been modeled after classical jūjutsu or its modern form, judo.

But the similarities are overshadowed by the differences. In aikidō, for example, there is no equivalent of grasping the opponent's sleeve or collar as seen in judo. Because there is no direct grappling and no competition, aikidō does not have offensive techniques. Nor does it have the same kind of floor techniques whereby the opponent is incapacitated by locks and neck holds.

Among the many similarities between aikidō and swordsmanship are certain fundamentals: the standing posture, the distance or space between two people, the placing of the eyes, the movement of the feet, as well as the derivative techniques, all of which are strikingly parallel, if not identical. While the judo costume is worn loosely because of the grappling, in both aikidō and swordsmanship the standard wear is the *hakama*, the long skirtlike formal wear of the Japanese, which suits the free movement of two people facing each other. (Kendo also uses the *hakama* but together with a variety of protective equipment. In aikidō beginners do not normally wear the *hakama*.)

On the other hand, a detailed comparison of aikidō and swordsmanship will reveal small differences. An example is the stance in distancing (ma-ai). In the art of the sword the proper space between two people is established when the tips of the two facing swords overlap slightly, so that one step forward would mean a lethal strike against the opponent. In aikidō when two people face each other in the *hanmi* posture, the hands, equivalent to the cutting edge of the sword, do not touch each other, and the space is adjusted for maximum efficiency in performing the entering (irimi) technique. Furthermore, in using the sword, regardless of how high or low it is held, the basic principle for determining distance is the same. In aikidō it will vary, depending on the technique; whether both partners are seated, one partner standing and the other seated, or both standing; one against many; or one against a person with a weapon.

In this respect we cannot establish a precise equivalence between aikidō and swordsmanship, but, as noted earlier, the basic principles, movements and methods of the two have much in common. The similarities did not arise by chance, for Master Ueshiba clearly intended from the very beginning to utilize the advantages found in the art of swordsmanship, and he devoted considerable time and energy to incorporating them into aikidō.

From his earliest years the Founder had a strong interest in swordsmanship. In fact, before he became engrossed in Daitō jūjutsu, he devoted himself to mastering swordsmanship. Even after establishing aikidō as an independent form of budō, he loved to practice with the sword and the *bokuto* (wooden sword). At one time, a kendo section was established in the Kōbukan Dōjō, and between 1936 and 1940 many leading members of the Yūshinkan, including Nakakura Kiyoshi, Haga Jun'ichi, Nakajima Gorōzō and others, frequented our dōjō. In my youth the Founder persuaded me to learn the art of the sword in the Kashima Shintō style, which also reveals his deep attachment and high regard for the art. In actively seeking to incorporate certain principles of swordsmanship into aikidō, perhaps he was attempting to develop a theoretical basis for aikidō, which was then still in its infancy.

Aikidō uses no weapon and is fundamentally an empty-handed martial art, but the hand, for example, is not just an extension of the body. Called the sword-hand (*te-gatana*), it becomes a weapon for striking, transforming itself into a sword. And when the hand is used as a sword, the movement naturally follows that of a swordsman. This is an example of an aikidō movement being a concrete manifestation of a principle of swordsmanship.

A classic example of this manifestation is the *shihō-nage*. The principle of this technique is patterned after the basic manner of handling the sword. Standing with either the left or right foot as the axis, the sword is wielded to cut in four, eight or sixteen directions. Using the basic aikidō techniques of entering and spherical rotation, the sword-hand is used to throw people in four, eight or sixteen directions.

This technique has infinite variations according to the situation and the need. When the attack is a blow coming from either the opponent's left or right side, the response is a shihō-nage to counter it. If the attack is grasping both wrists from the rear, one executes shihō-nage from this position. And if an attacker grasps the shoulder when seated, one defends himself with shihō-nage. Whatever the situation, shihō-nage essentially follows the same pattern. In the first stage the opponent's stability is upset by entering and spherical rotation. In the second stage the opponent is drawn into one's own circle of movement. In the final stage the right or left hand (sometimes both hands) is used as the sword-hand—raised above the head and brought down swiftly to throw the opponent.

Every move in shihō-nage is dictated by the awareness of employing the hand as a sword. This also means that the opponent's hand is regarded as a sword edge. Although neither party is armed, the action is as intense as it would be if naked blades were being used. Naturally, shihō-nage involves the concentration of ki for its power and effectiveness, and the flow of ki coming from breath-power is expressed fully through the hand—the cutting edge—that makes the throw sharp and powerful. Unless ki is flowing, the opponent will not be easily thrown.

Shihō-nage is considered to be the alpha and omega of aikidō techniques, and its perfection a sign of aikidō mastery. This is due to the fact that it most clearly embodies the principle of swordsmanship. This is the outstanding example revealing the intimate relationship between aikidō and swordsmanship.

Although aikidō is basically a weaponless art, and training typically consists of two people facing each other with open hands, applications of basic techniques using sword, knife, stick or staff are also found. In this case the reverse of using the hand as if it were a sword is found; the weapons are used and manipulated not as objects but as extensions of the body.

The foregoing should suffice to show the close relationship between aikidō and swordsmanship. But this is not enough to understand why the Founder incorporated the art of the sword in developing aikidō. In addition we should fully acknowledge the genius of the Founder in formulating aikidō, based on classical jūjutsu and the principles of swordsmanship, which were ostensibly different in nature. His originality lies not in merely combining the two but in founding a new form of budō that brought out the best in both.

The burning desire of the Founder in establishing aikidō was to keep the most valuable legacy of budō alive in the modern world. In order to accomplish his goal he went beyond differences in outward form to grasp the essence of each martial art and to bring it to life in a new form. The motivating force was his intense spiritual quest to discover a life-giving and life-affirming philosophy in budō. The result was the transformation of the heart of budō into the heart of aikidō, the way of harmony and love.

Strength in Living with Nature

The Joy of Practice

From the beginning aikidō preferred not to restrict students with too many rules and regulations. They were unnecessary, it was felt, because students came to the dōjō on their own initiative and most were seeking some goal through aikidō training. They could be expected to observe the proper mode of behavior.

This basic attitude upheld the principle of never refusing entrance to anyone who wanted to come and never chasing after those who departed. Those who came out of choice would naturally want to observe dōjō etiquette. Those who left would have no need for its rules and regulations. Rather than bind students unnecessarily, the tendency was to let events take their natural course.

One reason for emphasizing what was natural was the fact that when the Founder was first urged to open an aikidō dōjō, the original students were mature and experienced men of common sense who were acknowledged leaders in their fields. Being people with a strong sense of responsibility and decorum, there seemed to be no reason to subject them to codes of behavior in the dōjō. The Founder did not accept just anyone. He interviewed each person individually and was very selective. No outside factors could influence whom he would take as a student, and once a person was permitted to enter the dōjō, he met with the rigorous training program. In a sense, although students were not bound by rules and regulations, they were given a much heavier burden, but it was one they took on willingly because of the demanding discipline required in practicing aikidō.

Before long, with the great increase in the number of students, there were demands for dōjō regulations. On one occasion when the senior students went to see the Founder and made such a request, he smiled and said, "So, times have changed!" He then quickly wrote down the following six guidelines and handed them to the students. These became known as the "Reminders in Aikidō Practice."

1. Aikidō decides life and death in a single strike, so students must carefully follow the instructor's teaching and not compete to see who is the strongest.

2. Aikidō is the way that teaches how one can deal with several enemies. Students must train themselves to be alert not just to the front but to all sides and the back.

3. Training should always be conducted in a pleasant and joyful atmosphere.

4. The instructor teaches only one small aspect of the art. Its versatile applications must be discovered by each student through incessant practice and training.

5. In daily practice first begin by moving your body and then progress to more intensive practice. Never force anything unnaturally or unreasonably. If this rule is followed, then even elderly people will not hurt themselves and they can train in a pleasant and joyful atmosphere.

6. The purpose of aikidō is to train mind and body and to produce sincere, earnest people. Since all the techniques are to be transmitted person-to-person, do not randomly reveal them to others, for this might lead to their being used by hoodlums.

Since these were written around 1935, some of the language seems almost archaic, but the main points are valid today. In summary, they are: 1. Proper aikidō can never be mastered unless one strictly follows the instructor's teaching. 2. Aikidō as martial art is perfected by being alert to everything going on around us and leaving no vulnerable opening (suki). 3. Practice becomes joyful and pleasant once one has trained enough not to be bothered by pain. 4. Do not be satisfied with what has been taught at the dōjō. One must constantly digest, experiment, and develop what one has learned. 5. One should never force things unnaturally or unreasonably in practice. He should undertake training suited to his body, physical condition and age. 6. The aim of aikidō is to develop the truly human self. It should not be used to display ego.

These points are central to aikidō practice and are still upheld at the

Hombu Dōjō. Many people especially applaud the third item: "Training should always be conducted in a pleasant and joyful atmosphere." A common stereotype of martial arts is of the rugged, macho type with swaggering gait. But a display of bravado is evidence of ignorance concerning real budō and is, in fact, a childish attempt to conceal a lack of confidence. Those having true knowledge of budō are relaxed in bearing; they even give the impression of being soft and gentle. Those with confidence in budō never swagger or brag, and their demeanor is always pleasant and joyful. Outwardly they manifest gentleness; inwardly there is great strength. In daily life they are unpretentious and modest, and their actions are natural, never forced. They show themselves as they are, living life naturally and spontaneously. This is the picture of the true student of the martial arts. When such people gather for aikidō practice, the atmosphere is indeed naturally pleasant and joyful.

I have lost count of the number of aikidō practitioners I have come into contact with on a daily basis over the years. At the Hombu Dōjō alone there have been nearly 100,000 people, and if I include those I have taught in branch dōjō and other centers, the total would be several hundred thousand. It is a matter of pride that the vast majority practice aikidō with great seriousness and dedication. But when it comes to the question of how many truly enjoy a pleasant and joyful training experience, I cannot say that the number is that great. Many practice aikidō using excessive force, others with grim resolution, and still others lack confidence and practice very tentatively.

It is a delight to see practitioners who really enjoy their workout. Many have been practicing for five, ten or more years, following their own pace and making aikidō part of their daily routine. They appear at the dōjō, perform without much ado, throwing and being thrown, quietly following instructions, and leave when the class is over. They seem uninterested in promotion and have the manner of people who are enjoying themselves. They make the best aikidō students.

The regulars who attend our general practice or the summer and winter intensive training sessions thoroughly enjoy aikidō. The morning general practice at the Hombu Dōjō begins at 6:30 A.M. At that hour from late autumn through winter, it is still very dark outside, and in the middle of winter the temperature is below freezing. Yet from 100 up to nearly 200 regularly attend the morning classes.

Few of them live near the dōjō. The great majority commute daily by train for more than an hour or by car for 30 or 40 minutes. Some come from nearby prefectures and spend more than two hours traveling. Among the younger members, some use scooters or motorcycles, while others arrive at the dōjō after jogging for an hour or two. Then they all practice aikidō for an hour, after which they go on to school or to work. There are a few practitioners, some of them executives or proprietors of businesses, who have been doing this for a long time, and they say they do not regret missing a round of golf but they do not like to miss aikidō practice. Among the regulars are those who are never absent from a single day of practice.

A number of regulars attend every special summer and winter training session. They practice daily in the midsummer heat and humidity, perspiring profusely but training diligently, or come out every day in the middle of winter when a lengthy warm-up is necessary just to move on the ice-cold mats. For these people it seems that the hotter or colder it is, the better it is.

Several years ago I wrote an article for our aikidō newsletter, a few pertinent paragraphs of which read:

> This summer the heat has been terrible. Is that the reason we have had a 20 percent increase in attendance at our summer training session? It seems that there are many strong, hardy students at the Hombu Dōjō.
>
> I recall that in the winter training session when heavy snow brought public transportation to a standstill, some people got up at 3:00 A.M. and walked to the dōjō. The number of students present was almost the same as for a regular session. Among them were some who come to class irregularly but attended the special winter classes every day.
>
> Some really enjoy working out in the heat, perspiring freely, and others practice even more vigorously in the cold of winter. Common sense would dictate the opposite: normally people would prefer comfortable days to hot ones, and warmer temperatures to subfreezing weather. The people who prefer to experience the heat and cold tell me that it is the most direct way to experience nature. It may seem odd to outsiders, but I

can really appreciate their wanting to become closer to nature and to feel it at firsthand.

The Japanese word for practice or training is *keiko*, which literally means "to reflect, to go over the past." This word appears in the *Kojiki*, and its origin is said to be in the Kuan-ying biography in the Chinese *Book of the Latter Han*. The original connotes a religious quality in training consisting of respect for the best in old traditions and mastery of it by careful reflection and reenactment.

That keiko is central to the Japanese cultural arts, including the tea ceremony and flower arranging, evinces the respect the Japanese have for the best in ancient traditions. Midsummer and midwinter training is part of this great heritage. Using a rational approach, we might find arguments against practicing in extreme heat or cold, but if we do so, we will do nothing and forget about keiko.

Speaking of rational living, one of the products of modern civilization is the air conditioner. In Tokyo this year air conditioners recorded the highest sales in history, but the cumulative heat of thousands and thousands of air conditioner motors is said to have increased the air temperature by some degrees, resulting in humid and uncomfortable nights for most of the inhabitants. And the sudden change when going from the scorching heat outside into the chill of an air-conditioned room has caused some people to become ill. The fate of modern man is that in trying to solve problems rationally he creates many other problems demanding solution.

We all need to live rationally, but equally important for man is his need to become one with nature and allow mind and body to be cleansed and nourished by it. The real significance of early morning training and summer and winter special practice may be that it provides people with an opportunity to come into touch with themselves and nature. The practice of the martial arts which contains the best in traditional budō may be one way for all people to return to nature and find their roots.

The primary necessity is to recover our natural selves and bodies.

We live in changing seasons, in heat and cold, on clear days and rainy days. To truly experience nature is also to be our natural selves and know joy and anger, happiness and sorrow. When we resist or ignore nature, we find ourselves unable to truly experience the range of human emotions. This is part of the depersonalization and dehumanization that afflicts us all. We must return to nature, accepting it as it comes, and recover our natural selves and bodies.

A most satisfying aspect of aikidō is that there are many practitioners who are aware of this problem and are striving to recover their natural selves and their humanity through training. That goal has been at the center of aikidō practice from its very inception.

Absolute Nature: The Mutuality of Yin and Yang

Master Ueshiba constantly advised his students, especially those whose over-attachment to form confined their movements, as follows:

> In aikidō there are no forms and no patterns. Natural movements are the movements of aikidō. Its depth is profound and it is inexhaustible.

The meaning of the Founder's statement, frequently spoken in his personal, esoteric style, may not always be clear. For beginning students intent on mastering the different forms and techniques, his statement contradicts everything they are taught. If aikidō has no forms or patterns, what is the use of learning the different techniques? What is meant by natural movements? Can I move any way I want to?

The first thing to note is that the Founder's statement is not meant for beginners but for advanced students. It is advice directed to those who have attained a certain level of proficiency and yet are still so attached to form that they lack the natural, flowing movements that are the ultimate manifestation of aikidō. In a real sense, his words are meant to encourage advanced students to work harder until they attain the goal of aikidō. A classic Japanese proverb says, "Enter by form, and exit from form." Whether it be cultural arts or budō, one should train and master form, but having mastered it, one should become free of it. For those who have a long way to go to master form, it is not surprising that the Founder's words are confusing.

Full appreciation of the statement must be reserved for those who have truly trained and practiced aikidō for many years, who have mastered the principles and movements, and who have given considerable thought to the philosophy of budō. This requires both theoretical and experiential knowledge of the basic tenets of aikidō, including the unity of the ki of the universe and the ki of self, the principle of entering and spherical rotation with unified ki-mind-body, and the bodily manifestation of the principle of swordsmanship.

Perhaps the most difficult meaning to grasp is "natural movements." It is such a commonplace expression, and many people have some notion, however vague, of what it means. But seriously, how many people do we know who truly live "naturally"? The more we think about the connotation of "natural," the more difficult it becomes to explain it.

How should the aikidō student understand the meaning of "natural movements" and their relationship to the movements of his art? What is the key to unlocking its meaning, and where can we start? To give the conclusion first, I believe that it means to grasp within ourselves accurately and directly the working of nature which pervades the universe and affects our bodies and our lives.

Whatever we may think, it is crucial to come directly in touch with and receive openly the changes in natural phenomena—in atmosphere, weather and environment. In so doing we must bare our senses and bodies to nature and interact with it, neither forcing it to meet our expectations, nor selectively discriminating against particular aspects of it, nor utilizing it for our own purposes. We must see natural phenomena as they are and gain insight into the true nature of reality.

A concrete example may be found in the participation of students in intensive summer and winter training sessions. They constantly accept heat and cold as they are, enjoying the heat of hot days and the freezing cold of other days. When people experience heat and cold with their bodies, they learn how to react to them and come to know how well they can perform under uncomfortable or adverse conditions. This intimacy with nature and with one's body is the first step to mastering nature's ways.

It is a well-known fact that the weather affects our psychological state. On a bright, sunny day our minds are clear, our bodies light. The mood is one of quiet cheerfulness. On cloudy, rainy days our spirits tend to be low and our bodies sluggish. There is a somberness in the atmosphere.

On overcast days our minds and bodies are unsettled, and when the wind blows, a gentle breeze makes us feel good, while a typhoon causes agitation. Even on the level of such common occurrences we see the intimate relationship between nature and human beings. When it comes to more dramatic seasonal changes, it is not only the temperature and humidity that are affected. The life cycle of vegetation and animals also undergoes drastic changes. Plants bud, flowers bloom, leaves grow, fruits ripen, then all inevitably wither and die. Such changes have subtle effects on the human mind and body. We know for a fact that the changing tides govern the lives of marine life, and they have a subliminal influence on the way human beings feel and act. Volcanic eruptions and earthquakes wreak decisive changes in the life of the earth, which in turn sooner or later affect human life. All things in life are a vast web of interrelations and interdependence.

When we fully recognize how natural phenomena and their changes affect human beings, we also know that they are somehow connected to our own realization of the meaning of life. And as we come to understand and appreciate human life, we come closer to living together with nature and the universe. In this way, without losing our individuality and self-consciousness, we become one with the workings of nature. When this is accomplished, natural movements appear spontaneously in rhythm with the universe. This constitutes our understanding of what is natural. In aikidō it is manifested in the form of budō based on the active realization of ki. Herein lies the meaning of the statement, "Natural movements are the movements of aikidō."

The most important source of natural movements is breath-power. When breath-power flows spontaneously, a person's movements unconsciously become natural. In contrast, when breath-power is not freely emitted and the flow stops, movements become awkward and unnatural. The breath of breath-power includes normal respiration but it involves more than ordinary inhalation and exhalation, for it involves the working of ki.

Normal breathing is physiologically a function of the respiratory system centered on the lungs and heart and involving the nose, mouth and the pores of the skin. The human respiratory system is the most concrete manifestation of what we call life, and life itself is inseparable from the working of the universe. Thus, it is intimately connected with the cyclic changes of nature: night and day, the four seasons, the ebb and flow of the tides and other phenomena. Breath-power is deeply connected with the inherent power of natural forces and is expressed through the ki of the universe. The most elementary and concrete manifestations of breath-power in the movement of nature, as we have previously noted, are entering and spherical rotation.

Among the many natural movements in aikidō is the wrist technique known as *kote-gaeshi*. In this technique the wrist is bent slowly in the direction it naturally bends, unlike the wrist locks in judo and jūjutsu, where the wrist is bent in the opposite direction. Forced bending, being unnatural, runs the risk of causing injury. Aikidō never attempts movements that go against what is natural and thus avoids unnecessary and meaningless injury.

The majority of aikidō techniques have what are known as *omote* and *ura* movements (literally, front and back, respectively). Although there are differences according to the technique, the basic principle, for example, in countering a direct frontal attack is either to enter straight into the space occupied by the opponent, or to turn around and enter the blind spot behind the opponent to execute a technique. The former is an *omote* and the latter an *ura* movement.

These two defensive movements found in classical budō are based on the ancient principle of yin and yang, and aikidō also utilizes this principle in many of its techniques. Let us take an example each from jūjutsu and swordsmanship to illustrate the use of yin and yang in the martial arts. First is the definition of these terms according to a text of the Kitō school of jūjutsu:

> *Kitō* means rising and falling. Rising is the form of yang. Falling is the form of yin. One wins by recourse to yang and also wins by recourse to yin.

This is explained in the commentary known as *Densho chūshaku* as follows:

> When the enemy shows yin, win by yang. When the enemy shows yang, win by yin. The techniques taught in the Kitō School are limited to the use of yin and yang. Although countless other means are used to counter the enemy's moves, they are distract-

> ing in a contest. By limiting oneself to the techniques of yin and yang, victory is assured.

According to this explanation, strategy is nothing other than the ability to freely use yin and yang, offense and defense, depending on the way the enemy moves: counteracting his yin with yang and his yang with yin.

In the case of ancient swordsmanship, the principle of yin and yang was applied to the posture taken in holding the sword, as found in a text known as *Ittō-ryū kikigaki*:

> In the Naganuma Jikishinkage School they teach the posture of holding the sword high, this being the form of yang within yang. In the Ittō School we teach the posture of holding the sword low, based on the form of yin. When the yang within yang is used, it falls to yin. When our yin of yin is used, it becomes yang and works well. In the Munen School they take the middle between yin and yang, teaching the posture of holding the sword in front, pointing toward the opponent's eyes, but then twisting the hands slightly to the right.

The various schools of budō interpret yin and yang differently, but the interpretations are all derived from the basic philosophical ideas of classical Chinese thinkers. As a summary, we can quote a passage from the *Book of Changes*:

> In ancient times the holy sages composed the *Book of Changes* for the purpose of following the principle of nature and life. They established the Tao of Heaven and called it yin and yang. They established the Tao of Earth and called it the yielding and the firm. They established the Tao of Man and called it human-heartedness and rectitude. Combining these three powers, they doubled them. Therefore, in the *Book of Changes* the sign is always made up of six lines.

In brief, the universe consists of the three powers—Heaven, Earth and Man—and they are revealed as the Tao that operates in life through the relativities of yin and yang, the yielding and the firm, and human-heartedness and rectitude. This means that when we fully comprehend the working of these relativities and live in accord with them, we become united with the Tao. To manifest yin and yang in our actions is to be one with the Tao.

The principle of yin and yang has significance in itself, but ultimately it is through practice and realization that this principle enables us to attain the ultimate reality of the Tao. In aikidō yin and yang are concretely utilized in the omote and ura movements, but the fundamental point is that through practice one attains the Way and hence the fundamental truth. Since this is one with the Tao of Heaven, these aikidō movements are none other than natural movements.

Inheriting the Founder's Aspirations

A Brief History

Aikidō, the official designation, dates from February, 1942. Prior to that the art was known by various names, although the substance remained constant. A detailed history of aikidō may be found in the Founder's biography which I wrote in Japanese. (*Aikidō kaiso, Ueshiba Morihei den*. Tokyo: Kodansha, 1977.) What follows is a brief history tracing the name as it underwent changes.

Master Ueshiba's father, Yoroku, was a relatively prosperous landowner who also engaged in the fishing and lumber businesses. Respected by the people of his community, he served on the village and town councils of Nishinotani and Tanabe in Wakayama Prefecture. The young Ueshiba revered his father, and his father, seeing great potential in his son, gave him the fullest material and moral support to pursue his ambition beyond the limiting world of his birthplace. The son, however, felt that he had failed to meet his father's expectations and in 1901, at the age of 18, went to Tokyo, where he served a brief apprenticeship in the business world. The following year he started the Ueshiba Store, distributing and selling school supplies and stationery, but he became ill and his small business failed.

Not long after that he joined the Imperial Japanese Army and fought in the Russo-Japanese War (1904–05). He became a sergeant and received an honorable discharge. Then in 1912, when he was 29, he recruited 54 households comprising more than 80 people from his hometown and founded a new settlement in Shirataki, Hokkaido. The prefecture was then an area newly opened to development and welcomed settlers who would work the land. For seven years as the leader of this new colony, he cultivated the land, served on the town council, and contributed to the development of the Shirataki region.

Although he showed a certain talent for leadership, he still felt he had not realized his father's high hopes for him. The death of his father due to illness in January, 1920, came as a great shock to him. Leaving everything behind in Hokkaido, he returned home but experienced profound psychological distress. He then sought the guidance of Deguchi Ōnisaburō, the charismatic religious teacher of the Shintō-derived Ōmoto Sect. Under this great teacher's patronage, the Founder lived at the Ōmoto Headquarters in Ayabe, Kyoto Prefecture, practiced Shintō meditative and purification rites, and contributed to the strengthening of this new religion.

The eight years at Ayabe (until he moved to Tokyo in 1927) were formative years in the spiritual development of the Founder. During this time he studied Shintō philosophy and mastered the concept of *koto-dama* (literally, word-spirit).

After his father's death and during his stay at Ayabe, the Founder's dedication to budō became single-minded, primarily due to the encouragement of Deguchi. Prior to this time he had practiced and mastered several martial arts, including swordsmanship in the Shinkage School, jūjutsu in the Kitō and Daitō schools and others. Most remarkable among his accomplishments was his receipt of the highest certification in the Daitō School from Master Takeda Sokaku, whom he had met by chance at a Hokkaido inn in 1915, when he was 32. It was this jūjutsu that opened the Founder's eyes to the deep meaning of the martial arts; Daitō principles differ from aikidō's but many techniques are shared in common.

The reason Deguchi encouraged concentration on the martial arts was because he knew of the Founder's rich and varied background in budō and foresaw this path as the one most suited to his temperament, ability and aspirations. He advised the Founder to set aside a part of his residence in Ayabe and turn it into a dōjō. Taking this advice seriously, the Founder opened the modest 18-tatami Ueshiba Juku.

The Ueshiba Juku was originally intended for the young men of the Ōmoto Sect, but as the name of Ueshiba Morihei, "The Budō Master of Ayabe," became widely known, outsiders began to join the dōjō, the most prominent being young naval officers from the nearby port of Maizuru. His fame spread and students began coming from Tokyo and other distant parts of Japan.

From around 1920, Master Ueshiba had been seriously thinking about establishing his own independent form of budō, and in 1922 he proclaimed Aiki-bujutsu as a new martial art form. As the term *bujutsu* suggests, it retains the principles and techniques of older martial arts, which differ somewhat from present-day aikidō. His originality appears in the use of *aiki* as a specific term. There are scattered references in various budō transmissions to the idea of "matching" (*ai*) ki with the opponent in combat, but this was the first time for the compound itself to be used. There can also be found mention of *aiki-jutsu*, but this had a psychological connotation and was not an essential part of a martial art. In recent books a few references are made to an early modern form of *ki-aijutsu* popular among the common people, but this was a psychological system which had nothing to do with budō as such.

While choosing the new term *aiki* may have had something to do with the influences of the Kitō and Daitō schools, both of which are based on the principle of yin and yang and the use of ki, the fundamental source was Master Ueshiba's own budō training, life experience and the realization of ki gained during his stay at Ayabe. The most important influence was the mastery of koto-dama, which is referred to constantly in lectures, writings and instructions in his later years.

Aiki-bujutsu seems not to have been accepted immediately. Instead, people referred to the new budo as the Ueshiba-ryū or Ueshiba-ryū Aiki-bujutsu. Still, Master Ueshiba's fame continued to spread throughout the country. The turning point came in 1924–5, when, as noted previously, he went on an expedition to Inner Mongolia and soon after his return, when challenged by a young naval officer in Ayabe, experienced *sumi-kiri*, the clarity of mind and body that realized the oneness of the ki of the universe and the ki of self. He was in his early forties, and this became the foundation of his martial art.

We can say, then, that 1924–5 marks the beginning of the spiritual development of aikidō, for from this point on Master Ueshiba constantly advocated that "true budō is the way of great harmony and great love for all beings" and that every movement is the working of the unity of ki-mind-body.

In the autumn of 1925, after repeated requests by his patron and supporter, Admiral Takeshita Isamu, the Founder went to Tokyo to give a demonstration before a distinguished audience, among whom was the former prime minister, Count Yamamoto Gonnohyōe. Count Yamamoto was deeply impressed with the Founder's performance and had him conduct a special 21-day seminar at the Aoyama Detached Palace for high-ranking judo and kendo experts in the Imperial Household Agency. In the spring of 1926 he was again invited by Admiral Takeshita to Tokyo and gave lessons on aiki-bujutsu to members of the Imperial Household Agency, army and navy officers and leading figures in the political and business worlds. In 1927 at the urging of Admiral Takeshita and Deguchi Ōnisaburō, he left Ayabe for good and moved to Tokyo.

During the next three years he established a number of dōjō in the Shiba district of Tokyo and instructed many people in aiki-bujutsu, including high-ranking experts in other martial arts. There were signs of recognition of the Founder's budō as something more than the traditional martial arts, and some people began using the term aikidō to describe it. In October, 1930, Kanō Jigorō, the founder of Kōdōkan Judo, saw Master Ueshiba's superb art, acclaimed it the ideal budō, and even sent some of his best students to him.

In spite of attempts to be selective the number of students continued to grow, and the Founder had to face the need for a larger dōjō. In 1930 he established a new dōjō in Wakamatsu-cho, Tokyo, initially renting and later purchasing the property from the Ogasawara family. The new training center, called the Kōbukan Dōjō, was completed in April, 1931. As noted previously, the Aikidō Headquarters Dōjō now occupies the same site.

In 1936 the Founder decided the time had come to make the distinction between the old martial arts and his own clear, because of the philosophical and spiritual emphasis he had incorporated in his own art. Feeling that the essence of his new art was different from the old tradition of martial arts, he abandoned the term *bujutsu* and renamed his art aiki-budō. This necessary and inevitable step laid the foundation for the future of his school. As the founder of a new system of martial art, he strongly felt the responsibility to subordinate his personal quest and expand the way for all who might be interested in it.

In 1939 he submitted an official request for his organization to be recognized as a juridical foundation under the name Kōbukai. The approval of the request the following year made aikidō an officially incorporated body and marked the beginning of the Golden Age of aikidō. Membership grew and the name of Master Ueshiba became more widely known than ever.

The outbreak of the Pacific War in December, 1941, and the increasing shift towards militarism in Japanese society could not but hinder aikidō's growth. With the majority of young men being drafted into the armed forces, the number of aikidō students was greatly reduced. One of the government's moves in attempting to mobilize the country for the war effort was an order to unify the diverse martial arts groups into a single body under its control. In 1942 various traditions of judo, kendo and other martial arts joined together to form the Greater Japan Martial Virtue Association.

Although the Founder did not voice his objections to this government directive, it appeared that he was definitely unhappy that the budō he had developed as distinct from other forms was to be forced to become part of such an organization. Strongly opposed to being merged with other groups as just another martial form, he came to feel that the name Kōbukan Aiki-budō suggested that it was merely the Kōbukan branch or style of some broader art. He decided to proclaim the new name aikidō to identify his art as a unique and distinctive form of budō and then entered the association under the new name. In February, 1942, aikidō was officially recognized as the name of the Founder's school. Twenty-two years had elapsed since the birth of the Ueshiba Juku in Ayabe.

The Aiki Shrine at Iwama

To fully appreciate the proclamation of the name aikidō and understand some of the reasons behind it, including changes in the Founder's thought, we must turn our attention to the establishment of the Aiki Shrine at Iwama in Ibaraki Prefecture, northeast of Tokyo. This site, revered by all aikidō students, is especially important for the fresh beginning that followed World War II.

The idea of establishing a spiritual center for aikidō came to the Founder around 1935. It was born from a deeply felt need to continue the quest for the truth of the universe through budō, and he wanted a special place for this purpose. Having established a firm foundation for aikidō in Tokyo, his pure desire to spread true budō in the world was being fulfilled, and he took delight in the successes he had achieved. At the same time he felt dissatisfied with that alone, and in fact he seemed to deplore the invasion of privacy and the lack of time his fame had brought him. The Founder showed complete indifference to the normal objects of human desire—social position, honor and acclaim, wealth and material comfort. His sole concern was the training of the spirit through the discipline of budō.

Around 1935, making use of his small savings, the Founder began purchasing forest land in the countryside around Iwama. Farming was in his blood, as evident in his venture to colonize Shirataki in Hokkaido, and he planned to cultivate the land and renew the quest for a spiritual budō. But his wish to return to working with the earth could not be realized easily, for as a renowned martial artist he was constantly being invited to various places and his busy schedule left him no time to pursue his real desire.

The wartime attempt to organize all forms of martial arts under a single bureaucracy presented a unique opportunity. With events making it all but impossible to continue the normal activities of aikidō, he was no longer needed to direct its growth, and as the war clouds darkened, the number of his students decreased and invitations to perform aikidō declined. Undoubtedly, he felt that this was the ideal time for him to make a decision regarding his future. The order to join the Greater Japan Martial Virtue Association as part of the war effort was the last straw. Thus it was that the founder proclaimed the establishment of aikidō and finally made his decision to retreat to Iwama where he could pursue his own path.

The Founder was a patriot in the true sense, believing one should be willing to sacrifice his life for his country, and he chose not to protest the national wartime policy. Yet he disagreed with the move to unite all forms of budō under government jurisdiction; for him the directive had little to do with love of country. Moreover, the new organization demanded more and more paperwork and attendance at meetings, both of which ran contrary to his desire to continue his quest of budō.

With complete disinterest he would say, "I'm no good at paperwork. For me there's only the practice of aikidō." And so saying he would send one of his uchideshi, Hirai Minoru, to represent aikidō at the meetings. I was still a student at Waseda High School, but he appointed me chief instructor of the Tokyo dōjō and requested that his top disciples, such as Osawa Kisaburō, the present chief instructor, assist me. Then he left Tokyo for Iwama with my mother, Hatsu. This was done in a way typical of the Founder, who wasted no time in putting into action whatever he had decided.

Iwama is close to Mito, a center of learning and the arts during the Tokugawa period, but it was sparsely populated at the time. The farms were few and scattered, and the whole area was heavily wooded, 90 percent of it being covered with pine, fruit trees, and groves of other trees. The founder cleared about 20,000 *tsubo* (6.62 hectares) of the holdings he had acquired over the years and began cultivating the land, fulfilling his long cherished dream of unifying farming with martial art. The small converted farm building he lived in contained only two small rooms and one dirt-floored area. Visitors to this little hut were shocked by its shabbiness, but the Founder's spirits were high.

In settling in Iwama the Founder had in mind three plans to realize his ideal of a true budō. First was to establish an Aiki Shrine that would symbolize the Way of ai-ki and the spirit of aikidō. Second was to construct an outdoor dōjō permeated with the ki of nature where the ideal budō of *take-musu* could be taught. Third was to realize his cherished dream of unifying agriculture with martial art. He sought to relate the budō training (*take*) that harmonizes with the protective life force (*musu*) to the work of farming through which the earth produces life-sustaining food.

The Aiki Shrine was conceived to pay homage to the 43 gods who protect and give procreative power to aikidō and to be the sacred center for all aikidō practitioners who vow to promote the Way for all beings. The 43 gods refer to the martial deities, the dragon kings and the incarnations glorified in traditional Japanese lore. The Founder strongly believed that his prowess in budō came not from himself but from the gods that protected him and nurtured his ability. This was his ultimate faith, but more importantly it shows his humility and self-discipline: by entrusting himself to a greater power he would never become arrogant about his achievements. This humility, the epitome of his sincerity and devotion to training, is something all aikidō practitioners must take to heart.

The layout of the Aiki Shrine is based on the principles of koto-dama. The placement of the inner sanctuary, the hall of worship, the entrance gate and so on are all in accord with the three principles of the triangle, the circle and the square. These three signs are symbolic of the breathing exercise in koto-dama study. In the words of the Founder,

> When the triangle, the circle and the square become one, it moves in spherical rotation together with the flow of ki, and the aikidō of sumi-kiri appears.

That the Aiki Shrine, reflecting an elaborate philosophy, could be completed in the difficult years at the end of World War II was due to the efforts of a master carpenter named Matsumoto, who lived in Iwama, and the untiring support given by countless practitioners since the very beginning of aikidō. The completion of the main sanctuary of the Aiki Shrine in 1943 was an occasion that brought tears of joy to the Founder. His lifelong dream had been fulfilled, and the foundation for the future of aikidō was established. The shrine is now the mecca for all true students of the art.

The main celebration held at the Aiki Shrine every year on April 29 brings together aikidō enthusiasts not only from Tokyo but from all over the country and abroad. It is a festive occasion embodying the best in aikidō. I myself feel completely purified whenever I worship at this shrine and perform a demonstration.

Construction of an outdoor dōjō, the second part of the Founder's plan, took place in one corner of his farm. But with the increase in students, it was necessary to build a small indoor dōjō of 30 *tsubo*. This was completed in 1945, immediately after the end of World War II. It diverged from the original goal of combining agriculture and martial art, but it brought unexpected benefits to aikidō.

During the three years after the war, the Hombu Dōjō at Wakamatsu-chō was forced to curtail activities for a variety of reasons, including the ban on all martial arts imposed by the Allied Occupation Forces. All the activities of the central dōjō were then moved to Iwama, so that at a time when the general climate and mood towards martial arts was strongly negative, aikidō was able to endure because of its dōjō at Iwama. Today, it is called the Ibaraki Dōjō, and is dedicated to the memory of the Founder.

The Founder had long cherished the ideal of establishing an Aiki center. That this was accomplished, albeit with minor changes, in the midst of the difficult war years and chaotic post-war years was almost a miracle. It must have been very gratifying to the Founder to be able to escape the busy life of Tokyo and devote himself totally to realizing the ideal of true budō.

The road to recovery for aikidō began in February, 1948, with the official approval of the Aikikai as the new juridical body. It was first seen publicly at the Takashimaya Department Store in Tokyo in September, 1956, and the First Public Aikidō Demonstration, sponsored by the Aikikai, was held in May, 1960, at Yamano Hall in Tokyo. The peak of the post-war revival came with the completion of the new Hombu Dōjō in January, 1969.

Seeing the prosperity that aikidō has attained, I cannot help but reflect on the decisions made by the Founder during the war years and immediately thereafter. Had Master Ueshiba, instead of retreating to Iwama, let Kōbukan Aiki-budō be swallowed up in the merger of the martial arts during the war, the history of aikidō might have ended at that time. Both the names of Master Ueshiba and aikidō, and their brief but glorious chapter in budō in the prewar years, might have been relegated to the history books and with time become only obscure legends in the annals of the martial arts.

Aikidō's reputation and success today are due to the Founder's decision to devote himself to a spiritual quest for the essence of martial arts in the hinterlands of Iwama. Master Ueshiba demonstrated by his own example that the prosperity of aikidō is not measured by the number of followers but by the depth and intensity of the personal quest for truth through training and practice. This, I believe, is the major reason for aikidō being what it is today.

The Zen saying, "Reflect on our footsteps," admonishes us to always see whether or not our feet are on solid earth. As aikidō practitioners, we must always "Reflect on our footsteps," even as we move forward together with high idealism and a passion for truth.

There is nothing more desirable than growth and expansion, but if our eyes are attracted only to surface events and we lose sight of the essence of the Way of aikidō, then—just as a spinning top loses its momentum, its balance, and sooner or later falls—our Way will lose its vitality, become divided, and eventually disintegrate. When I think of the years the Founder spent in Iwama reflecting on himself, I am again reminded of my essential task.

The Founder giving a demonstration at the Aiki Shrine in 1962.

The Founder demonstrates *shōmen uchi* (front strike) at the Noma Dōjō, in Tokyo in 1936.

Variation of *irimi-nage*. (Noma Dōjō, 1936)

Demonstration of *kokyū-nage*. (Noma Dōjō, 1936)

Demonstration of basic techniques in Wakayama, Wakayama Prefecture, in 1951: *kokyū-nage*.

Demonstration of *kokyū-nage*. (Wakayama, 1951)

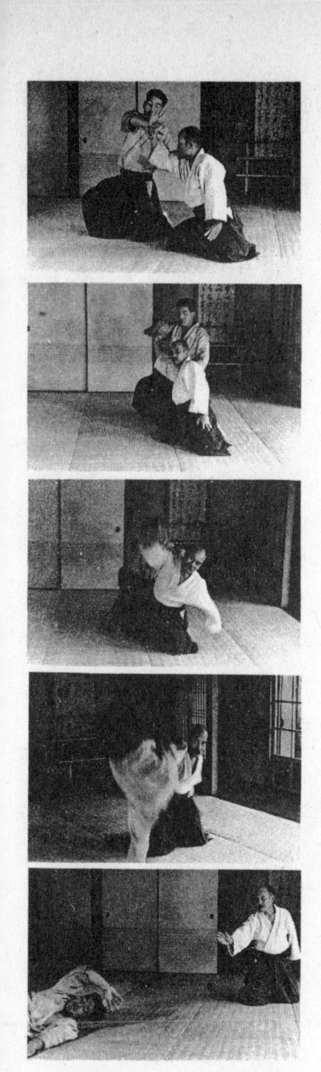

Demonstration of *kokyū-nage*. (Noma Dōjō, 1936)

Demonstration of *kokyū-nage*. (Wakayama, 1951)

Irimi-nage combined with a front strike. (Noma Dōjō, 1936)

Demonstration of *hanmi handachi* (oblique facing, half standing) *shihō-nage*. (Noma Dōjō, 1936)

Master Ueshiba on a day of relaxation at the Aiki Shrine, Iwama, 1962.

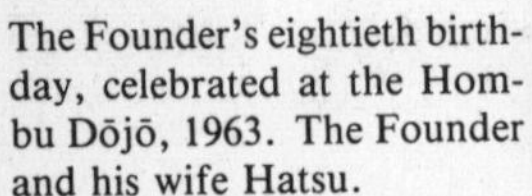

The Founder's eightieth birthday, celebrated at the Hombu Dōjō, 1963. The Founder and his wife Hatsu.

Aikidō Takes Roots in the World

Internationalization and Tradition

The Third Congress of the International Aikidō Federation was held in Paris in 1980. Delegates from all over the world discussed and unanimously endorsed the internationalization of aikidō, with the center being the Hombu Dōjō in Tokyo. To be sure, the atmosphere during the four-day congress was charged with enthusiasm for this ambitious undertaking.

Most gratifying was the delegates' reaffirmation that aikidō embodies the best in the spiritual culture of Japan. They not only acknowledged the uniqueness of aikidō, but also recognized its philosophical basis deeply rooted in Japanese tradition. In fact, a majority expressed the view that their interest in aikidō was directly related to the fact that it represents the best in Japanese culture.

I mention this because I have been concerned for some time with the way traditional Japanese martial arts have developed abroad. When they are transplanted to another country, some of the martial arts seem to lose their distinctive, traditional roots and become only a matter of physical skill. In the end the center of the art shifts to the countries that develop physically strong and technically skillful contestants. I cannot agree that this is an inevitable part of internationalization. As far as aikidō is concerned, the uniqueness of Japanese philosophy forms its essence, and my conviction is that anyone who disagrees with this is no longer an aikidō practitioner. The meaning of internationalization is not that the unique tradition becomes internationalized, but that aikidō practitioners in every country should change and unite with the tradition.

All during the congress I expressed my concern to delegates from various countries, and I believe the majority accepted and supported my view. This is probably due to aikidō's being primarily a spiritual path which decries any form of competition or tournament where victors or vanquished are decided and everything hinges on winning.

The tournament system is the root of the problems arising with the internationalization of Japanese martial arts. While tournaments have played a definite role in spreading the martial arts throughout the world, they also suppress the unique quality of budō (as opposed to bujutsu), whose primary concern is the cultivation of the spirit. When strength determines all, Japanese martial ways lose their true essence, and it is only natural for physical skill to take stage center. When that happens Japan abrogates its claim to having developed a unique martial art concerned not with violence and brutality but with peace and love.

I reiterate this point because I do not want to see aikidō repeat the mistakes of the other martial arts that have spread throughout the world. I am, of course, most grateful for the selfless efforts and sacrifices made by the aikidō instructors who have propagated the seeds of the art in various countries of the world. The spread of aikidō began in the 1950s in France, Hawaii, New York and other parts of the United States and continued in the 1960s in England, Italy, Brazil, Argentina, Australia and Southeast Asian countries. I welcomed these developments, but I could not respond immediately to the many invitations to visit the foreign centers of aikidō, primarily because of the above concern.

After carefully weighing the matter, I concluded that we could proceed if we first clarified two main points about aikidō: the essence of aikidō is the unique Japanese philosophy which affirms the spiritual quest as the first principle of budō and the tradition founded by Master Ueshiba is the only true form of aikidō. As long as we can accept and affirm these two principles, we can avoid the errors seen in the spread of the other martial arts. And as long as we preserve aikidō's rejection of competitive tournaments, we will not lose the integrity of true budō.

These points were clearly in focus when we deliberated the possibility of forming the International Aikidō Federation in Madrid in November, 1975. The first general convention of the International Aikidō Federation was held in Tokyo in October of the following year, and as of 1981, the federation consisted of forty member countries and more than 100,000 practitioners, 20,000 in France alone.

The Third Congress of the International Aikidō Federation in 1980 was a truly significant event signaling the dawn of a new age for worldwide aikidō. Personally, as Dōshu, that event was very encouraging for the support I received regarding my concerns and my ideas for the future development of international aikidō.

Looking through the newspapers after I returned to Japan, I came across the following article in the *Nihon Keizai Shimbun* (September 30, 1980). It said in part:

> The burgeoning interest in the Japanese martial arts is truly amazing. At first it was only judo, but today there are aikidō and karate dōjō everywhere with everyone from the common people to intellectuals enjoying the practice sessions. For five days from today (September 30–October 4) a congress of the International Aikidō Federation is being held in Paris. Delegates from forty countries in Europe, North and South America, Southeast Asia, etc. have assembled, and the public demonstration on the third day is expected to draw 5,000 spectators.
>
> Why is Japanese budō so popular? In the case of aikidō it is not a combat sport to see who wins, and anyone—middle aged, old aged, women, children—can fully participate in it, which makes it attractive to those who want to do some kind of exercise for health reasons. More important, however, is its appeal for nurturing etiquette and proper behavior, aspects not found in Western sports, and for the Oriental mystique found in waza, which totally involve one's body and mind.
>
> The secret of Japanese economic success is that, whether it's electronics or automobiles, the goal is to master the basic technique, and having digested it completely, to come up with something new. What supports this endeavor is the spirit of harmony and cooperation that is ai-ki. We hope that this essence will be transmitted to Westerners at the meeting of the International Aikidō Federation. However, the Japanese must remember that pride goeth before a fall.

I thought the journalist was very perceptive in his comments on the Western interest in aikidō. I myself have felt for a long time that the primary attraction has been the emphasis on "etiquette and proper behavior,'' my impression being that the majority of aikidō practitioners have the correct understanding of the place of etiquette and proper behavior and of what is referred to as ''Oriental mystique.'' Not everyone, of course, has reached that level. There are differences in cultural background, and the general appreciation of such matters as they pertain to the essence of aikidō may be higher among thoughtful Japanese students. Yet I can safely say that among Westerners there are some who show a greater intensity in their quest for the spiritual in budō than does the average Japanese involved in aikidō.

Among French practitioners, there are many who have been deeply immersed in Zen training and look to aikidō as a dynamic form of Zen. In England students and graduates of Oxford, Cambridge and other universities show great sympathy for the ideals of aikidō manifested in its world-view and mind-body integration. Many students I have met in the United States seek in aikidō training a key to self-identity, and in Germany some see the essence of the Japanese spirit in aikidō and believe that it can contribute to breaking through the impasse faced by Western civilization. There has been a sudden surge of interest in aikidō recently in Southeast Asia. One of the reasons seems to be the belief that the strong spirit cultivated by budō may have contributed to Japan's economic prosperity, a phenomenon viewed with both amazement and envy.

These are merely abstractions of my impressions of why people in different countries take an interest in aikidō; they are not the result of any objective surveys. In truth, I have yet to accurately grasp the reasons for the interest. Still, having spoken to foreigners both at the Hombu Dōjō and during my many trips abroad, my impressions may contain some truth.

It seems to me that many who have entered the gates of aikidō have done so not directly but in a circuitous way. That is, many are impressed by Japanese spirituality, characterized by harmony and cooperation, and they turn to aikidō, which appears to best symbolize this. And once they begin training, they learn about the unity of self with one's body, nature and the universe and become lifelong students.

Such an approach to aikidō fosters a highly intellectual appreciation of its essence. Perhaps this is due to the fact that among Westerners aikidō tends to draw educated, thoughtful people, and because they are intelligent, they grasp aikidō both in its particularity—the highest expression of Japanese spirituality—and its universality—the beauty and rationality of aikidō movements.

The future of aikidō is assured as long as all practitioners, Japanese and foreign alike, endeavor to train rigorously and strive to realize spiritual cultivation. When both are done, then we may contribute our share to making this world a better place for ourselves and our children. For that, after all, is the aim of true budō.

A Bridge to Peace and Harmony

At the time we felt deep concern about the proper promotion of aikidō throughout the world, Master Ueshiba shared his view on its becoming international in the following way:

> That will be wonderful. Aikidō is the bridge to peace and harmony for all humankind. The first character for martial art, *bu*, means "to stop weapons of destruction." If its true meaning is understood by people all over the world, nothing would make me happier. The creator of this universe, which is the home for all humankind, is also the creator of aikidō. The heart of Japanese budō is simply harmony and love. It's only natural that everyone would welcome it.

Some of the Founder's favorite poems reflect the same thought:

Ai-ki, the root
Of the power of love,
Makes love grow
Forevermore.

The great universe
Is itself the Way of ai-ki—
A light for countless peoples
That opens up the world.

This beautiful form
Of heaven and earth
Is a single household
Created by the guardian spirit.

The Founder was invited to attend the opening ceremony of the new central aikidō dōjō in Hawaii on February 28, 1961. He was already 78 years old but he boarded the plane in high spirits. At his farewell party, he gave a short address, the gist of which was:

> The reason I'm going to Hawaii is to build a Silver Bridge of understanding. I have been building a Golden Bridge within Japan, but I also wanted to build bridges overseas and through aikidō to cultivate mutual understanding between East and West. I want to build bridges everywhere and connect all people through harmony and love. This I believe to be the task of aikidō. But I am still in the process of training, so I want not only to build bridges but to delve more deeply into the heart of true budō. True martial art which I call take-musu aiki embraces all beings in love and works for the peace of all humankind.

Short though his statement was, the Founder expressed what all students of aikidō must aspire to: working for the well-being of all humankind, promoting love and peace, and at the same time plunging ever more deeply into training and practice with the aim of realizing the true essence of the universe. I take this admonition seriously, especially at a time when aikidō appears to be prospering the world over. I want to constantly strive in training, day by day, and thereby demonstrate the real value of aikidō.

That aikidō enjoys a sound reputation and has won the admiration of people as an ideal form of budō is due to the strivings of the Founder and the pioneers who laid the foundation through dedication to training. Aikidō survived the vicissitudes of recent history because of the stress on achieving its spiritual goal through disciplined practice. But where we are at this point in history is only a stage in an evolutionary process, and we must take care to insure its continuity in the uncertain future. We can do that as long as we cherish the spirit of aikidō, the art of love and harmony that is also the heart of universal reality.

Appendix: World Aikidō Directory

Aikikai World Headquarters
International Aikidō Federation
17-18 Wakamatsu-chō
Shinjuku-ku, Tokyo 162

ARGENTINA

Katsutoshi Kurata
Esmeralda 1385 PB "G"
Cap. Fed., Buenos Aires

Kenzo Miyazawa
Juan de Garay 2244 Olivos.
1636 Pcia. de Buenos Aires

BRAZIL

Reishin Kawai
Brazil Aikikai
Rua Geraldo Amorim No. 98
05594 Jardim Bonfiglioli
Sao Paulo

Makoto Nishida
Av, Leonardo da Vinci-38
V. Guarani S.P. CEP, 04313

Ichitami Shikanai
Rua Florenca 75, Sta Terezinh
Belo Horizonte M.G. CEP. 31360

CANADA

Fumio Ishiyama
Victoria Aikikai
P.O. Box 5581, station B,
Victoria, B.C.

Yukio Kawahara
Vancouver Aikikai
Box 1102-151-4800
Kingsway, Vancouver, B.C.
V5H-4J2

Osamu Obata
108 Wishing Well Dr.
Scarborough, Ont.
MIT 1J5

ENGLAND

Minoru Kanetsuka
British Aikido Federation
155 High Rd., willsden Green
London NW10 2SG

FRANCE

Nobuyoshi Tamura
Chemin des 4 Platanes
83470 St-Maximin

ITALY

Yoji Fujimoto
Aikikai Milano
Piazza Toscana 2
Pieve Emanuele

Hideki Hosokawa
Via Istria 140
09047 selargu (CA)

MALAYSIA

Jun Yamada
P.O. Box No. 592
Kuching, Sarawak

NEW ZEALAND

Nobuo Takase
P.O. Box No. 11-241
Ellerslie, auckland

SPAIN

Yasufusa Kitaura
Fernando el Catolico, 71-5°, Izgder
Madrid 15

Takeji Tomita
Aikido Dojo Stockholm
Kommendörsgatan 29
114 48 Stockholm

SWITZERLAND

Masatomi Ikeda
Bäckerstrasse 27
8004 Zürich

THAILAND

Motohiro Fukakusa
Thailand Aikido Association
No. 79, Soi Akkapat Sukumvit
Sukumvit Rd.
Bangkok

UNITED STATES

Kazuo Chiba
San Diego Aikikai
3760 Fairmount Ave.,
San Diego, CA 92105

Mitsunari Kanai
New-England Aikikai
2000 Mass. Ave.
Cambridge, Mass. 02140

Akira Tohei
1318 W. Norwood St.
Chicago, Ill. 60660

Yoshimitsu Yamada

Seiichi Sugano
New York Aikikai
142 West 18th St.
New York, N.Y. 10011

Ichiro Shibata
Berkeley Aikikai
1812 San Pablo Avenue
Berkeley, CA 94710

Mitsugi Saotome
Aikido Schools of Ueshiba
421 Butternut St. N.W.
Washington D.C. 20012

GERMANY

Katsuaki Asai
Aikido-Schule
Augusta Str. 36
40477 Dusseldolf 30

Glossary

ai, harmony, 19
atemi, strike, 18

bodhimanda, place of transformation of ego self into egoless self, 10
bokuto, wooden sword, 80
budō, Way of martial arts, 7
bugei, fighting arts, 7

dō, Way, 19
dōjō, place of enlightenment, 10

funakogi, boat rowing (exercise), 53
furitama, ki settling (exercise), 53

genki, vigor, 22

hakama, long skirtlike formal wear, 79
heiki, equanimity, 22

iki, will power, 22
irimi, entering, 18
irimi-issoku, entering with a single step, 41

kaiki, recovering life, 22
kaiso, founder, 96
kami, deity, 9
kan, intuition, 73
kata, form, 7
keiko, practice, training, 88
kenjutsu, swordsmanship, 79
ki, fundamental creative principle (force, energy), 11, 15, 19, 21
kisoku, prolong breathing, 22
kitō, rising and falling, 22
kokyū-hō, breathing method, 26
koto-dama, word-spirit, 97

ma-ai, distancing, 18

nage, one who leads, 53
nen, concentration, thought-moment, one-pointedness, 36

omote, front, 92

seiki, spirit-energy, 22
seiza, formal style of sitting, 53
shihō-nage, four-direction throw, 78
shikaku, dead angle, 41
shiki, courage, 22
shikko, seated movements, 53
shinogi, ridge on sword blade, 73
shūki, conserving energy, 22
suki, opening, 8
sumi-kiri, clarity of mind and body, 38
suwari-waza, floor techniques, 53

tai-sabaki, body movement, 18
take-musu, martial-creative, 75

MARTIAL ARTS

THE ESSENCE OF AIKIDO

Spiritual Teachings of Morihei Ueshiba

Compiled by John Stevens

A complete collection of the writings of the founder of aikido, and a master guide to aikido technique. Hundreds of rare photographs of Ueshiba in action.

Hardcover: 200 pages, 182 x 257 mm, ISBN 4-7700-1727-8
Paperback: 200 pages, 182 x 257 mm, ISBN 4-7700-2357-X

BUDO

Teachings of the Founder of Aikido

Morihei Ueshiba   Introduction by Kisshomaru Ueshiba

Morihei Ueshiba wrote this treatise on the martial arts for his advanced students in 1938, outlining the spirit and aims of aikido. Illustrated with rare photographs.

Paperback: 132 pages, 182 x 257 mm, ISBN 4-7700-2070-8

THREE BUDO MASTERS

Kano (Judo), Funakoshi (Karate), Ueshiba (Aikido)

John Stevens

The first comparative study of the lives of the founders of judo, karate, and aikido and their profound influence on modern society.

Paperback: 176 pages, 113 x 188 mm, 15 b/w photos, ISBN 4-7700-1852-5

THE UNFETTERED MIND

Writings of the Zen Master to the Sword Master

Takuan Soho

The philosophy and competitive strategy presented by the spiritual mentor to Musashi is as useful to today's corporate warriors as it was to 17th-century samurai.

Paperback: 104 pages, 110 x 182 mm, ISBN 0-87011-851-X

HAGAKURE

The Book of the Samurai

Tsunetomo Yamamoto   Translated by William Scott Wilson

"A guidebook and inspiration for any modern student of martial arts, or anyone interested in achieving a courageous and transcendent understanding of life." —*East West Journal*

Hardcover: 180 pages, 128 x 189 mm, ISBN 0-87011-378-X
Paperback: 180 pages, 110 x 182 mm, ISBN 4-7700-1106-7

KENDO

The Definitive Guide

Hiroshi Ozawa

The first truly comprehensive guide to kendo features easy to follow line drawings to demonstrate techniques, basic information on equipment and lists of official rules and clubs. For beginners and experts alike.

Hardcover: 244 pages, 182 x 257 mm, line drawings, appendices, ISBN 4-7700-2119-4

KYUDO

The Essence and Practice of Japanese Archery

Hideharu Onuma, & Dan & Jackie DeProspero

A fully illustrated guide to the spiritual and technical practice of this graceful martial art, by a 15th-generation master. Detailed illustrations and rare photographs.

Hardcover: 176 pages, 182 x 257 mm, 4 color plates, 86 b/w photos, over 300 illustrations, ISBN 4-7700-1734-0

ILLUMINATED SPIRIT

Conversations with a Kyudo Master

Dan & Jackie DeProspero

In an inspirational dialogue with the authors, kyudo master Hideharu Onuma explains the fundamentals of breathing, posture and discipline, and points the way to an inner calm, focusing on the here-and-now, and gaining a greater understanding of one's own mind and body , as well as the world around.

Hardcover: 160 pages, 128 x 188 mm, 45 b/w photos, index, ISBN 4-7700-1970-X

STICK FIGHTING

Techniques of Self-Defense

Masaaki Hatsumi & Quintin Chambers

A manual of self-defense techniques using a long or short stick. Shows some 50 moves, each clearly demonstrated in photos with step-by-step instructions.

Paperback: 148 pages, 148 x 210 mm, 250 b/w photos, ISBN 0-87011-475-1

COMPREHENSIVE ASIAN FIGHTING ARTS

Donn F. Draeger & Robert W. Smith

The classic, unrivaled guide to all of the main fighting arts of Asia. The authors introduce and compare fighting methods and techniques ranging from the artful Chinese *t'ai chi* and Japanese *jujutsu*, to the lethal *pentjak-silat* of Indonesia. Over 200 photos and drawings.

Paperback: 248 pages, 182 x 257 mm, ISBN 0-87011-436-0
Previously published as *Asian Fighting Arts*